DILLIBE ONYEAMA

AFRO SAXON

HOMECOMING MEMORIES OF A

BLACK BOY AT ETON

adrant Books

Quadrant Books

Republished in 2023 by Quadrant Books
A member of the Memoirs Group
Suite 2, Top Floor, 7 Dyer Street, Cirencester, Gloucestershire, GL7 2PF

A catalogue record for this book is available from the British Library.

AFRO-SAXON
Paperback ISBN 9781739864538

Printed and bound in Great Britain

Dedication

This book is dedicated to the praise and worship of the sacred name of the Crucified, and to the inspiration and honour of his most virtuous mother the Virgin Mary, and to the maintenance of the glorious profit of his holy Church.

Contents

Preface

This is a book of reminiscences and musings, triggered by the events which created them, which are faithfully recorded herein. None of the events purported to be true are the result of invention, exaggeration or figments of the imagination. They all took place. It should be assumed that the style adopted in their presentation was intended to reflect (it is hoped) an eye for aesthetics, an ear for dialogue, and an appetite for the ancient craft of story-telling.

The essence of this book is to entertain and provoke a few thoughts. The inspiration came from the gales of laughter that greeted some of those experiences recalled, as well as the tears of ire that sometimes drowned out those of amusement. In the analysis of good and evil, one is confronted at the end of the day with the civilized duty of saying the nastiest things in the nicest way. That is what diplomacy is all about – although a school of thought teaches that the principal function of a diplomat is to speak French and to tell lies. But the story that follows is presented in the best English diction that it is within the author's capacity to express, and so expressed with nothing less than a strict regard for truth.

Dillibe Onyeama

Introduction

May it please that Yours Truly be accorded the privilege of introducing himself. He was the *Nigger at Eton*, and wrote about it. Fifty years later that title was diluted to the more diplomatic *A Black Boy at Eton*. In their respective eras both titles provoked controversy of near-volcanic proportions.

One should say the story merited telling – if because of the eccentricity of such a choice for a British scholastic system that was created by English royalty to provide for an already selected minority of the British society a privileged education that equipped them to fulfil their purpose, predestined by birth, as pillars of the ruling class and leaders of the establishment.

Moreover, when the status of the British private school reached its zenith during the era of the British Empire, it was producing the very people who were most needed to show the flag and spread the word of British power and wisdom among the so-called 'backward' peoples in whose lands the crown had already established acquisitive occupancy. Hence the eccentricity of the choice of a pupil south of the Sahara as an ideal candidate for such an education is eloquently emphasised. "Really letting the side down," founder King Henry VI would most certainly have grunted as he turned in his grave.

The sub-Saharan pupil, out of his depth as the only cup of coffee in the place weakened by milk, albeit of supreme quality, would at any rate find blessed solace in the truism that his membership of this exclusive breed of humanity would (or should) read well in his *résumé*. He may not have the facial features to look the part when cocking a snook in the nose-in-the-air English snob tradition, nor the gaudy garments of black tail-coats and striped trousers designed for pupils a cut above the English crowd, but he would at least luxuriate in the supreme quality of *almost* every feature of his career in this exclusive world-famous breeding ground of dignity, courtesy and culture – a breeding ground which had produced some of the world's most distinguished men.

There was supremacy in the quality of education, supremacy in privileges made in heaven, supremacy in sports, supremacy in charity work, in recreation, in cuisine. One felt that had it been possible, the English aristocracy would have privatised fresh air for its mollycoddled angels.

This sub-Saharan pupil's dusky appearance attracted insults in generous doses of variety. But he could not call the school a racist institution: if it had been, he would not have been there in the first place. He could not indict his tormentors for being colour prejudiced. They would just laugh it off with the defence "Some of my best friends are coloured." No – what he could legitimately lay claim to was the very definite existence of supremacist attitudes that ran like a thread through the soul of English royal disposition – sometimes deployed with hostility, sometimes with patronising, tongue-in-cheek love, sometimes with the constant arrogance of ignorance, sometimes with shallow atheistic stupidity.

The satisfactory breaking of many jaws in response could not rival the scale of insults and jeers, if only because of the greater population of white over black; but at any rate there was the feeling of giving as good as one got: "You insult my black face, I break your white jaw."

It was a terrific adventure (or misadventure) that would serve to instil a deep sense of colour-consciousness for the departing sub-Saharan pupil, notwithstanding the corresponding sense of accomplishment bestowed by his privileged plunge into the unfathomable depths of English finesse. In the profit and loss account, one could talk, grudgingly, of overall profit – in terms of quality education, the corresponding insight into human relations, and the comfortable feeling of confidence of being above it all and able to hold one's own in any situation anywhere in the world.

But still, at the end of the day, there was one glaring fact: no way could any member of the Caucasian groups of humanity consider his sub-Saharan counterpart as his equal, except possibly before God.

In the light of these observations, it is easy to draw an inference that the worth of the aforesaid royal education, apart from the basic privilege of its acquisition, would be of relevance for the sub-Saharan pupil *only* if he elected to reside in Britain, or Australia, or New Zealand, or Canada, or the USA – those nations ruled by powers that represent kith and kin to the English. The name of the school alone is like a magic wand that provides an automatic passport to gainful employment in any of those countries. In the developing sub-Saharan communities, however, whose comparatively unlettered citizens are possessed of a get-rich-quick mania, it counts for nothing, and would indeed present a stumbling block to the customary sharp practices which, by and large, are a way of life. Our molly-coddled intellectual could drown in frustration, destined ultimately to want to return to the greener offshore pastures that refined him.

CHAPTER 1

Tears for a Publisher

The book originally titled *Nigger at Eton* was the fallout of experiences hinted in the foregoing passages. The lava from the earthquake it caused has still not fully set. The British ruling class was hardly amused. I was banned from darkening the school's hallowed corridors in the wake of a serialisation of the book in a popular London magazine, and the ban was renewed when the story was subsequently published in book form.

If the often salacious farrago of sex, snobbery and racism that formed the ingredients of the two-part magazine serialization upset the school's governors, it got worse when more juice appeared in the book. The determined efforts to frustrate its publication must be recorded here, if only to offer insight into the savagery of the very rich.

Tears have to be shed for the good old publisher, Leslie Frewin, a quintessential Englishman if ever there was one. Beefy, in his mid-50s, his bushy eyebrows enhanced the impression of an astute, all-knowing sage, but his vaguely comic facial appearance, with his striking resemblance to the great comic Oliver Hardy, belied his true character. He was as tough as he was disarming with his infectious charm. But be stroppy to him, and he would be stroppy back with compelling rhetoric that befitted his calling as a man of letters.

My author-publisher relationship with Frewin was formed in the wake of the aforesaid serialisation and the subsequent ban on him from visiting the school as endorsed in a letter by the Headmaster, the late Michael McCrum. I rebelled against this ban on a matter of principle as opposed to any real feeling of slight. The school had been battered over the years by tearful *exposés* of unwholesome practices, but no ban was imposed on any of the milk-coloured Old Boys. I sought the support of British Peer Arthur Gore, the 9th Earl of Arran, Member of the House of Lords. An Old Etonian, he authored a weekly write-up in the London *Evening News* – 'The Arran Column'. It was popular because he thrived on laughter at his own expense and in the process earned the nickname 'Boofy' – a dilution of the buffoonery he acted out in his lively and hard-hitting observations on current affairs.

Before his Lordship could agree to grant me audience, he phoned to ascertain my exact reasons for wanting to see him. "If it's a job you're looking for," said he slowly, like one fishing, "I haven't got one. If it's money you're looking for, I haven't got..."

"No, no, it's none of those, sir."

"Oh I see – you want to come and kill me," he guffawed with his notorious 'boofy' riposte.

I got to see him and complained of the injustice of the ban. He phoned the following day after careful thought. "No, no the headmaster shouldn't have banned you. He had no right to do that. If you go to the Race Relations Board, he would be in terrible trouble."

"Yes, sir, I think I will do that."

His lead story in his next column announced a sensation: "The

Headmaster of Eton, Mr. Michael McCrum, is in danger of being reported to the Race Relations Board." Blah blah blah... "It's clear that Mr. Onyeama had to put up with a lot, what from being asked if his mother had a bone through her nose... Eton headmasters have an arrogance all of their own, and I would have thought it the height of unwisdom for Mr. McCrum to issue his ban. I only hope he obtained legal advice before doing so."

The story triggered a media sensation when my petition was finally filed before the Race Relations Board. But, characteristic of the Old Boy Network, the initial response was somehow predictable. "It seems to us that any pupil who writes such a damning indictment against his school would most likely be banned. Which is to say that the reason you were banned is not because you are black, but because of the vexatious nature of what you wrote. It is only on the point of that former consideration that the Board would be prepared to act."

But none of my milk-coloured Etonian forerunners who endorsed scathing criticisms of the school for world public consumption, most notably David Benedictus in his earth-shattering novel *The Fourth of June*, were subsequently banned. Was my hide not milky enough? Such was the contention presented in his reply – which went unanswered.

When the charge was finally rejected, there was no real disappointment: more satisfaction that additional spotlight had been cast on his coming book on his *alma mater*. "You can't win them all," guffawed Lord Arran again on the phone. "At least you made your point. But does your mother, in fact, have a bone through her nose?" he guffawed again in his notorious tone of child-like farce. Ha ha ha!

Sparing no effort to try to prevent publication, the indefatigable

Michael McCrum telephoned publisher Leslie Frewin, saying, "Look, old chap, couldn't you just drop this book? Boys will be boys, and this is really nothing more than small boys poking fun at each other." To which Frewin replied that if it was as trivial as he was making out, there should be no need to go to such an extreme as cancelling publication.

McCrum was a tall gentleman, strikingly handsome, distinguished by hair that greyed at the temples, and with an imperious mien that was enhanced by the rather haughty manner with which he puffed on his pipe. This was counter-balanced, however, by a small, effeminate voice that must have given him a terrible complex because it presented the unedifying impression of a woman in a man's body.

Inadvertently McCrum shot himself in the foot when a *Sunday Times* news and camera crew, with Yours Truly in tow, visited him to ascertain the school's official attitude to the imminent publication of the book. After a cool, composed and superior effort to appear the soul of reason against Yours Truly's persistent claims of racial intolerance, he declared finally, "We have another good little nigger boy here now, and he is perfectly happy."

The *Sunday Times* team returned in triumph to their headquarters to make a feast of their scoop, but not before it was leaked to *Private Eye*, which gleefully published a story about the use of the 'n" word by the Headmaster. McCrum wrote an instant denial saying "Nigger – never use the word. Apology please." Not that he never 'used' it during that taped interview, but subsequently, conveniently, he did not 'use' it now that his possible 'slip of tongue' had been accorded the indignity of public exposure. The public's interest in the book, understandably, rose to fever pitch.

"If he had been *really* intelligent," remarked Leslie Frewin of McCrum, "he would have gladly invited you with open arms to visit

Eton at any time. That would have placed a strain on the credibility of your charge of racism. But by imposing a ban instead, he has effectively reinforced the veracity of your claim."

Privileged information in due course revealed that the Headmaster was not operating on his own initiative to try and suppress the book. The 'Voice of the Palace' among the Provost and Fellows, Eton's Governing Board, was acting on instructions from colleagues among the 'Powers behind the Throne'. That was high-powered Old Etonian Peter Alexander Rupert Carington KG, GCMG, CH, MC, PC, DL (of blessed memory), 6th Baron Carrington, Conservative politician and hereditary peer, war veteran, former Secretary of State for Foreign, Commonwealth and Development Affairs of the United Kingdom, former 6th Secretary-General of NATO. Here was a poker-faced specimen whose bespectacled, surly façade featured a smile on the rare occasion when diplomatic good sense compelled him to flash it and get it over and done with.

It was widely perceived that it was Carrington who took Margaret Thatcher to hand and, in decisive military lingo, counselled and guided her on how she should play the role thrust upon her of 'Iron Lady' as Prime Minister. He it was, too, who confronted his Nigerian opposite eyeball-to-eyeball on the lawns of Lusaka during a Commonwealth Heads of Government Meeting (CHOGM) and engaged him in a shouting match over Nigeria's seizure of the assets of Shell-BP.

From all accounts, His Lordship likewise saw red over the idea of a book titled *Nigger at Eton*. One did not need to stretch one's imagination to suspect a 'supremacist' fire that fuelled his rage over such a perceived dent to the integrity of British royalty.

The next challenge to Leslie Frewin came in a letter from Lady Ann Fleming, wife of James Bond creator and Old Etonian Ian

Fleming, threatening to send Frewin to hell if any mention was made of her son Caspar in the book he was publishing on Eton. The said Caspar was my old contemporary at the school, in the same house. He featured in my work as a journalist as the anonymous culprit in an exclusive story for the *Sunday Express* about a loaded gun being found in an Eton boy's bedroom and police being called in to investigate. Though Caspar (now of blessed memory) was never identified by name, nor prosecuted, he was compelled to leave the school in quiet disgrace. Lady Ann Fleming, distraught over fears that the sordid details and family name would be laid bare for uncharitable world public consumption, minced no words in her threat to Frewin – who, undaunted, reserved his rights in this matter with an economy of words that summarised the dimness of his view of the complainant.

The next scene of drama came from the City Sheriff of London, *demanding* - as opposed to requesting – the book on Eton. Get it on publication day, he was told. We want it now, came the answer. Not possible.

"That's not the safest thing to say," was the counter. "Perfectly safe," answered the man of letters. But Frewin was not completely unperturbed, as was reflected in his tone on the phone to me. "It's a rather high-powered firm of lawyers," he confessed cagily.

A month before publication, a terse Sheriff came on the phone with a tone of reprimand. "I gather you have sent out review copies."

"Routine," he was told.

"I haven't received my copy yet."

"I'm not aware I ever said I was going to send one to you."

"Jolly unsporting of you, old boy, don't you think? Let me remind you of the Broome versus Cassell & Co Ltd libel case in which the jury awarded Broome £40,000 in damages being the highest award for libel made in England. So – watch it."

Frewin, dismissively: "Oh, I've known Captain Jack Broome for years and I'm probably far more privy to the case than you will ever be."

"Very well, old boy. I should say it is better to sort all this out now. It could be rather expensive for you."

"I will worry about that when we get to it."

"Very well. Should I interpret that to mean you won't be sending the book?"

"Buy it on publication day."

The book weathered all the pre-publication storm and saw the light of day with great hullabaloo. At a birthday banquet a top-ranking Old Etonian marquis with royal connections declared, "Leslie, I shall never forgive you for publishing that book."

Another old boy of my generation waded in with a vociferous denunciation: "That book is just a bundle of bloody lies. Nothing like that ever happened."

Frewin, his feathers characteristically unruffled, quoted Voltaire's philosophy with cool composure: "I may hate what you say, but I shall defend to the death your right to say it."

But the grizzled old publishing guru was never let off the hook for that perceived slur on the integrity of English royalty, and pro-royal figures in both the press and the public never let him forget it. Leading the pack of potential crucifiers was popular satirist John Wells (of blessed memory) whose review in *Punch* magazine, 'Eton People is Wrong', was a full page of unapologetic bombardment on the head of dear old Frewin. I quote: "*Nigger at Eton* incidentally, we are told on the black and white dust jacket, with the black and white Minstrel-style eyes rolling up through the two capital G's of '*Nigger*', jacket design copyright Leslie Frewin Publishers 1972, 'is the author's own title of his work'. Incidentally, that is, in case cynical persons should suspect the said L. Frewin, who was, incidentally, the publisher of *The Wit of the Duke of Edinburgh*, of exploiting the author's titillating predicament in a sensational manner for base personal gain. The author himself, in a brief preface, clears the air: 'But for the encouragement and advice of one in particular (a good friend who wishes to remain anonymous), I would never have had the inclination, patience or endurance to re-write it'. Indeed, even with the encouragement and advice of one in particular, Leslie F., who does not wish to remain anonymous, few people will ever have the inclination, patience, endurance or £2.70 necessary to buy it. And on the strength of African opinion to be found in the book, presumably untainted with the particular type of black-white racial prejudice thrummed into such Frewinesque crescendos throughout, he does seemed possessed of the uninhibited larger-than-life bounce of an African Billy Bunter... There is certainly no reason to forgive the tiny hooligans for racially abusing their victims. There is even less reason to forgive the man Frewin for encouraging his author to racially abuse himself."

But good old Frewin took it all in his stride, throwing the buck back at the reviewer like one dismissing the irritant behaviour of an incorrigible child: "People like Wells survive by looking for scapegoats to cover their own peculiar complexes and failures. Wells' problem is that he invested almost all his life's savings in a project that didn't quite come off. That's his trouble."

I myself did not completely escape the ire of several members of the English elite. The three hostile reviews of my book paled into insignificance against the multitude of glowing *bons mots* from both sides of the Atlantic, and it was clear that the extreme right wing members of the old boy network felt he had gotten away with too much, that the ban on him was not effective enough. This was reflected, in due course, during the earlier stages of the on-line social network communication novelty, when a full feature write-up in *Yahoo Mail* was devoted to deftly analysing my literary efforts. In the initial paragraphs it conveyed the impression of objective impartiality, and then, like a bolt from the blue, in the tradition of the accomplished matador, it ended by driving in the fatal arrow to score 'bull's eye': "There are so many people who wish Onyeama could have disappeared, quite frankly."

It was not difficult, painstaking as it was, for me to compile a list of fifteen people I knew for sure I would have wished off the radar. It is a striking fact that, in the course of time, I would be reading the obituaries of eleven of them.

CHAPTER 2

John Bull's nigger

Following the aforementioned experiences, I could not help but devote keen interest to the vexed subject of 'the black skin' on the global horizon. As a former imperial power that ruled over half of the world, Britain offered the ideal scenario for me to be able to explore and drink in the complexities of a multi-ethnic society with a greater variety than most countries.

Invaluable insight was offered by the windfall of my employment as an external paid critic for the highbrow London-based literary magazine *Books & Bookmen*, charged with the exclusive privilege of reviewing books on Africana and race relations in general. My bookshelves groaned under the weight of some 50 books acquired over a period of eight years on these subjects, and by the time I had studied them I felt I had become something of an authority on both – as much on the hideous details of 400 years of the Western slave-trade as on the no-less vexed issue of the Colonial experience in Africa.

I was naturally motivated to identify with the plight of 'my kind', feel their pains, and – allowing for recognised bias – view the discrepancies between black and white from a black perspective.

During my three years of hostel accommodation in West London, a generous sprinkling of well-educated African students presented the ideal *camaraderie* for lively intellectual intercourse on the black experience. Regrettably, the feeling of brotherhood ended there. It did not extend to the West Indian population that had elected to make Britain a permanent home, apparently unaware of the absurd hypocrisy of their eternal claims of white exploitation in their Caribbean homelands; for, in contentedly taking menial jobs which their white British hosts considered beneath their dignity to touch, they were in effect being subjected to further exploitation.

Most African students would head for home after their studies. Most West Indians in Britain would stay put as second-class citizens, but in the latter case, there was a need for some measure of understanding. The ready-made 'utopia' that Britain offered would not readily be shunned by third-world subjects seeking a better life, even as second-class citizens. The alternative that their homelands had to offer by comparison could not bear thinking about – let alone the pains of returning.

Still, the two groups, Africans and West Indians, eyed each other warily from a distance, the Africans contemptuous of the others' second-class status and their refusal to return to build up their homelands, the West Indians no less disgusted by the Africans' 'primitive' third-world posture in the comity of nations. Dialogue between the two groups was scarcely above a whisper, most of the time. It was a disquieting scenario that made a mockery of the concept of a united front to fight colour prejudice.

While there was a tacit understanding of the patriotic duty not to condemn one's own in the hearing of the perceived 'enemy', it seemed to me that it was precisely through such open 'chastisement' that any hope of sanity could be brought to bear.

On Speakers' Corner, West London, that Sunday soapbox where speakers such as Orwell and Marx have tried to convert the masses and now peopled mainly by Black Power orators of an often rash and fiery temperament, a small group of noisy blacks were avidly reminding themselves: "We blacks are all the same: Americans, Africans, West Indians – we're all brothers. We all have the same cause. The white man is our common enemy."

Joining the debate, an Asian visitor observes, "It's all very well to say you're all brothers, my friend. What about the time when Ghana threw Nigerians out of the country? Where was the brotherhood in that?"

A pot-bellied African cuts in with a kind of theatrical declamation: "Ah, but you see, wherever you get trouble between a black man and a black man, the white man's influence is dangling."

This was the popular mind-set: that the white man was responsible for every 'black' ill. I was inclined to consider the matter in a different light, seeing an emerging dangerous trend from this unwholesome scenario. Having been the victim of a flawed racist myth that the black man could do no right, a new myth was now being peddled that he could do no wrong. If he, in turn, starts to subscribe to such an erroneous notion as a sacred truth, and holds fast to it, the final outcome for any form of truce on the tensions that have divided the two racial groups becomes a remote dream.

There could be no truth in the idea that black prejudice did not count. Black prejudice *did* exist – it *was* being enacted in diverse forms. When President Idi Amin of Uganda expelled his country's Asian population, and later meted out the same treatment to the Jewish population and subsequently butchered an estimated 50,000 of his own citizens on ethnic grounds, barely a whisper of condemnation came from any sector of the world, let alone the United Nations.

When President Jean Bedel Bokassa of the Central African Republic demanded the most severe punishment for petty thieves in the form of cutting off their ears in public, sometimes their hands, and then later butchered 100 secondary school children for demonstrating against his rule requiring them to buy school uniforms, likewise there was a conspiracy of silence from the world. The Organization of African Unity (OAU) raised only a brief eyebrow at the event, because it would not be proper to be indicting fellow African Heads of State in the face of the racist animosity being practised as a way of life by apartheid South Africa, Rhodesia and Namibia.

With that show of reason, the world was expected to mind its own business – and did mind its own business – over the hideous torture chambers in Hastings Banda's Malawi, the blood-letting perpetrated by soldiers of Zaire's Mobutu Sese Seko, and the murderous reign of terror enacted by the Tonton Macoute in Papa Doc Duvalier's Haiti. But then when Amin provoked neighbouring Tanzania in his attempt to annexe Tanzania's Kagera region in 1978, President Nyerere finally lost his cool and ordered his troops to invade Uganda in response. Tanzania's army and rebel forces successfully captured Kampala on April 11, 1978, and ousted Amin from power into eternal exile in Saudi Arabia, where he finally died. Did Nyerere then stand to be indicted for overthrowing a fellow black African?

These excesses could be appreciated, if they *were* appreciated, only by those white supremacists whose irrational prejudices against the black man needed confirmation. Nobody cared so long as the inhumanity was being perpetrated against fellow black people.

On the strength of these considerations, I felt compelled, with corrective motives in mind, to commit to paper dissenting views on the notion of 'his people's implied exemption from well-balanced and constructive dissuasion from attitudes and behavioural patterns that would not help their cause'. That cause was legitimate when seen in the light of the fact that while all the other races in the world fought wars over politics, ideology, property, land and border disputes, the black man's colour was the sole reason for the global mind-set to dehumanise him. Accordingly he had no option but to rise and organise on the basis of colour to fight that oppression. But the approaches being applied to engage meaningfully in that fight, by first destroying his own, were hardly cricket. It was a cause for shame. A compassionate school of thought did volunteer the defensive argument that no room was left for a downtrodden people to demonstrate individual initiative except through cut-throat dog-eat-dog activities from within their own group.

The book *John Bull's Nigger* was the sequel to *Nigger at Eton*, penned with a possible palliative in mind to help to address a gaping wound. It backfired, throwing a lighted match into a pool of fuel that sent many personal 'black' instincts running riot. A prominent leader of the Community Relations Commission, one Lewis Chase from the Caribbean, went for the jugular of the publisher – poor old Leslie Frewin again. The press did not spare Frewin either. The *Sunday Telegraph* denounced him with the charge that the author "has become one more victim of the race relations industry". Chase filed a complaint to the Commissioner of Police, who sent a uniformed officer to the well-appointed offices of the publisher to purchase a copy of the book and obtain a receipt.

Not done yet, Chase notified the police of his intention to lead a picket to the offices of the publishers, who were alerted and advised to keep their front doors locked. Every 20 minutes from morning through to the close of business hours, the crunch of boots on concrete sounded as a dozen police officers marched through the narrow passage siding the publishers' office in anticipation of trouble from picketers – who never showed up.

Chase mounted endless pressure on the Director of Public Prosecutions to take legal action against the publishers, backed by a host of well-placed white sympathisers. His complaint was centred on the strong language employed in the book as being obnoxious and, even if taken out of context, capable of inflaming racial tensions. We talked on the phone several times, and failed to reach accord on the question of how motive and intention on my part could in any way be interpreted as a conspiracy to flout the Race Relations Act.

I understood that it was pointed out to Mr. Chase that he could not effect retribution against the publishers without the author being also answerable. His contention was that I 'published' the manuscript to the publishers, as it were, and they published it in commercial quantities, well aware of the danger the contents of the book posed to race relations.

The press made a meal of it. Frewin was at his wit's end. I was singularly unconcerned. Frewin phoned to report that he had it on good authority that the Director of Public Prosecutions was preparing to file charges under the weight of considerable pressure to do so. Frewin was uncomfortable. I felt for him, but he himself was not intimidated. On the contrary, he was intrigued, bemused, to see how any charge of colour prejudice against him could be sustained with any hope of success.

He called me to his offices to say, "It does look as if you and I could be sitting as guests in one of Her Majesty's prisons charged with conspiring to inflame racial tensions."

"Oh dear," said I, feigning concern.

"Which firm of lawyers are you going to brief to defend you?" Frewin wanted to know, clearly hoping to hear that they would both join forces to put up a fight.

"I don't propose to waste a brass farthing on any lawyer," I told him. "I will defend myself, even with misplaced confidence that I will win."

I really could not have cared less. It seemed the strong points which the prosecution would attempt to use to buttress its claims would be passages of perceived inflammatory language. This would be countered by my humble admission of lacking the Shakespearean literary skills to present my critique with love and warm kisses. They would say my first published literary effort, *Nigger at Eton,* was embarked upon when I was still a toddler aged only 18, completed when I was still a toddler at 19, submitted to the publisher when I was barely out of toddlerhood at 20, and published when I was on the brink of adulthood at 21. *John Bull's Nigger* followed two years later, having been penned even before the first book was published.

That line of defence could be further substantiated by two of the only three hostile reviews of my first book, one by influential journalist Katharine Whitehorn on a TV panel discussion on new books: "Eton clearly did not teach him how to *write!*" Another was by an apparently enraged critic with *The Scotsman* who suggested that the book "would be regretted more by his former English teacher than his school governors".

Hence, as age verified, Yours Truly was still a mere novice in the literary arts – by virtue of which – *inter alia* other considerations - it would be well-nigh impossible to prove the existence of a conspiracy to flout the Race Relations Act.

I found the courage to phone and speak to the Director of Public Prosecutions directly, to ascertain from the horse's mouth what exactly might be my fate. The Director accorded me the privilege of agreeing to take my call, and then proceeded to condemn *John Bull's Nigger* in the strongest terms. He concluded by saying, "Obnoxious as we found the book, we've decided that we are not going to press charges." He then paused, as if waiting to hear my response. Then he blurted out, "You sound disappointed."

Well – that wasn't entirely a lie. One could call it a terminological inexactitude. It would have been astonishing if a case resting on such flimsy grounds as would be put up by the Prosecution would not subsequently break down before the court.

It didn't all end well, however. For Frewin there was surely a sigh of relief, but for me there were well-articulated invectives from members of the black community, together with an enraged midget at a nightclub taking a swing; I was saved from being eaten alive by the intervention of peacemakers. Mother Time in due course proved to be the ultimate arbiter, relegating the matter to history. But an invaluable lesson gathered therefrom defied the settlement of dust with a powerful message: that though education is a good school, the fees are high – the highest being Truth. And to tell the truth, one must have one's foot in the stirrup. I was no bronco-buster.

Comforting as it was to assuage my despondency over being something of a loser in the fight to project truth as in the case of my second book, it was backed up by another powerful consideration rooted in divine law. "ALL have sinned," an eccentric orator at Speaker's Corner, Hyde Park, quoted from the Holy Book as a reminder to his audience; "and all have fallen short of the glory of God." The fundamental premise of this message is that all men have done enough to be ashamed of, and no one, be they black, white, yellow, brown or red, has a monopoly of righteousness. While this truism tended to trivialise the challenges of colour prejudice and man's inhumanity to man in general, the final message presented evil as a personal issue inherent in the observation that a man's toothache means more to him than a famine which may be killing a million people in some offshore location.

Caught in the unedifying crisis of jumping from the frying pan of English elite grooming into the flames of comparative third-world mediocrity, there was the questionable comfort that this was just the beginning, early stages yet, and that Mother Time would usher in the ideal compromise to balance out one's equilibrium. This more comforting hope, predicated on the reality that hope often proved to be a good breakfast (but just as often a bad supper), took cognisance of my determination to face any challenge, of any nature and magnitude, anywhere in the course of life. Such an invaluable dividend had been provided by Eton, my *alma mater*, establishing in the process an impenetrable fortress of confidence that could offer no excuse for failing to meet and overcome any challenge eyeball-to-eyeball with supposed 'superior' intelligence.

CHAPTER 3

An Englishman's castle

At this juncture, this story involves a transatlantic trip down memory lane for a brief encounter with the people around whom the guts of my story revolve.

We are off to Britain, an island of advanced people of Caucasian/Aryan extraction who talk strictly because they have something to say, and not because they have to say something; where the national philosophy is that it is better to keep quiet and be suspected a fool than to speak and remove all doubt; and where the *modus vivendi* proclaims that talk would be supremely improved by the perennial use of the three simple words "I don't know."

Hence the only true conversation with an Englishman, wait for it – is *SILENCE*.

I discovered this the hard way. At the age of nine, in the spirit of true African deference, I addressed a strict anti-social schoolmaster for whom it seemed to be an affliction even to smile by saying, "Good morning, sir."

"Good morning!" came the sharp, unfeeling dismissal.

I persisted the following day: "Good morning, sir."

"And a very good morning to you too!"

Day Three: "G-G-Good morning, sir."

"Look, will you please mind your own business!"

The culture of minding your own business well represents the true English trademark. There can be little dispute that silence in that context is one of the hardest arguments to refute. It is also the greatest weapon of war, proclaimed French strongman Charles de Gaulle (of blessed memory). Need one then question the claim that Britain rules the waves?

From that cultural silence emanated virtues that paved the streets of London with the finest gold. There was thus created an organized welfare society that guaranteed a lifetime of absolute peace to anyone of peaceful disposition. These virtues honed every indulgence into a fine art, epitomised every moral virtue, and established traditions of dignity, courtesy and culture.

Challenged Barbara Walters of screen fame: "Show me someone who never gossips and I'll show you someone who isn't interested in people."

How true of the Englishman. Yet curiously, in that lack of interest in people lies a magnet that draws members of *Homo sapiens* from all corners of Mother Earth to the bright lights of London like so many moths. In fact, at Christmas only, out of the twelve months of the year, do the British *pretend* to be human; and in the intervening period, any meaningful development in conversation with a now-familiar stranger will centre, much of the time, on the weather. "Cold day, isn't it?" is the favourite inane observation from every other pair of Anglo-Saxon lips. Or otherwise, "Beautiful day, I say" – sometimes three or four times a day. As British weather is pretty rotten ninety per cent of the time, this is no mean assault on the ear-drums in the name of conversation.

In my brainwashed naivety, on returning to Africa for those first summer holidays aged nine and proceeding to apply this quaint fashion of greeting to my fellow countrymen, I showered daily praise on the ever-present sunshine, in the same vein vilifying the occasional instance of downpour. "Is this child going mad?" was the response. But in the case of the British, it may not have been quite madness: you could call it benign eccentricity. Puffed up, for instance, by their technical and scientific progress, their intellectual power has metamorphosed into atheism: why, they have put themselves in the place of God, taking the bull of misapplied knowledge by the horns rather than waiting for God's own time – which avowed Christians insist is the best.

Other touching varieties of English eccentricity see women placed on the pedestal in the social order, frequently sitting at the head of the dining-table during meals. Animals are often more glorified than people – demonstrated by the tendency of every other mother to leave babies in prams outside on the pavement while shopping and take their dogs inside. Everybody on the scarred face of Mother Earth is a foreigner except the Englishman, explaining why "the wogs begin at Calais" (I'm sure, to the eternal delight of the Frenchman). And the English spirit of compromise would have you believe that injustice, when it is halved, becomes justice.

For twenty-two years I lived and breathed the benign eccentricity of these supremely-gifted islanders, and in those twenty-two years, I was accorded the privilege of exposure to (and acquaintance with) every imaginable race, hue, creed and faith on Mother Earth. To enhance the glory of such a privilege came the tolerance of the host natives whose imperial adventures across the seas had attracted the world to England in the first place. They had to grin and bear it; for the craved wholesale repatriation of those multitudes of overcrowding and stifling alien ways that now threatened to despoil in totality the near-perfect virginity of the English paradise was not really feasible in the face of the lucrative investments that had accrued from those imperial adventures on the global markets offshore. As ye sow, so shall ye reap, ha ha.

The aliens spared no mercy for those responsible for the anti-immigration waves of discontent from elements of Mother Country. Slurs, jibes and taunts were freely swapped, each side giving as good as it got. The hosts' contention was, "Why not go back to your country and do some good?" The riposte was: "Oh blessed interloper on the colonies, you went fishing beyond your own territorial waters, which had only coalfish with which to feed you, for an over-abundance of manganese fish, goldfish, oil fish, gas fish, timber fish, diamond fish, sugar fish, steel fish, tea fish, aluminium fish – every imaginable kind of fish that enriched our waters. You cast your net too far and too wide, and caught us into the bargain. Suffer us, therefore, we pray – to pursue and ultimately to survive on the milk from our soil, to wherever it might have been relocated, until we have properly mastered from your teaching skills the art of fishing, so that we may go home and be fed for life."

There was a strong case, fair judgement, on both sides. But, still – all is vanity. From that vanity sprouted the personal stories of many an alien who lived and breathed the Anglo-Saxon experience, and who, yielding to the prick of conscience to go back home and do some good with all that wealth of exposure to 'new world' refinement, suffered the titillating and potentially rewarding theme of the purgatory of reintegration into 'alien' ways. It became a well-worn theme, told and retold on the premise that no personal story, like the signatures and prints on the palm of the hand, can ever have a duplicate. In consequence, the bookshelves have never ceased to groan under the weight of data.

But why come back? Why suffer the shame of defeat by returning to old territory? What was wrong with the home-grown spouse with whom you returned to settle down out of patriotic duty, having discarded like old overcoats the 'colonial' angels of bliss in the ready-made paradise of London? Your people laughed at you when you started wearing a bowler hat in the tropics (unable as you were to shake off that English gentleman fever), and your English gentleman laughed even louder when you showed up again in London donning an exotic kaftan as some make-believe identity-tag. You had to drop out of your former circle of friends because you no longer had a natural identity. Your English gentleman walks with an erect bearing of home pride, as does your own back home, while you are grovelling with one foot in London and the other in your native environment south of the Sahara, as if stricken with acute constipation.

And your story, which you endorsed in book form and were rewarded with larger-than-life fame, big money, praise to high heaven (serving also as a means of getting that bug of being lost out of your system and offering some sort of redemption) – were you not also aware that it was a confession of sorts? Had you forgotten Josh Billings' counsel – "Confess your sins to the Lord, and you will be forgiven; confess them to men, and you will be laughed at"?

But never mind: those who laugh have not yet heard the bad news. Moreover, if you fail to master the art of laughing at trouble, for sure you will have nothing to laugh at when you are old. And in all those repetitious 'love stories' on the crisis of reintegration and self-rediscovery, there was invariably one vital thread of human iniquity missing that not only compromised both the bad news and trouble, but performed the function of locking the whole mystery of man's origin and his relationship with the Omnipotent into an instantly understandable whole.

In that way, this particular story may differ from its predecessors. In the distracted yo-yoing between London and the 'Third World' in search of one's true human identity on the treacherous path of hopelessness, one was not prepared even to consider the fiendish but thought-provoking remedy from German-Jewish poet Heinrich Heine. "If thy tongue offend thee, tear it out," said he, in echo of the teachings of the Omnipotent in the Holy Book. "If thine eyes offend thee, pluck them out. If thy hand offend thee, cut it off, And if thy brain offend thee – turn Catholic."

Aha! Given the innate weakness of the human flesh against much-abhorred threats of physical dismemberment, only a negligible few (myself counted amongst them) have shown any disposition to entertain the last option, the others electing, instead, to sample the seemingly less traumatic and covert alternative of gentle psychiatric counselling (they failed to observe, incidentally, that anyone who visits a psychiatrist needs his head examined).

The decision to pursue the Catholic remedy followed in the wake of one's inadvertently, instinctively, treading the atheist path of the Englishman, and discovering – to one's chagrin – the increasingly suicidal danger of remaining on that path. Whoever tells you that evil is transformed not into an angel of light? Oh my, all those steamy days of sin in paradise, masquerading as pleasure, freedom and enlightenment. Home sweet home, here we come; all is forgiven. Now, some half a century later, prayerfully sanitized, hopefully purified, faithfully rooted in the fertile home soil of 'Third-World' existence (that faith entrenched even more in the gracious hands of Catholic Providence which facilitated the miracle of difficult things taking a long time, the impossible a little longer), one has a much clearer picture and appreciation than your average 'Afro Saxon' of the collective madness fuelling human vanity – and the Englishman's contribution to that madness.

When the Englishman's brain continued to offend him even with the sanctuary of Catholicism, he turned Protestant, remember; and that option yielding no dividends either, he embraced scientific logic for his very life – which favoured the expedient attitude that going to church did not make you a Christian any more than going to the garage makes you a car (Laurence J. Peter must be acknowledged for that sagacity). G.K. Chesterton put it more succinctly: "Christianity has not been tried and found wanting; it has been found difficult and left untried."

Hence, with that offensive brain tumour in dogged persistence, the Englishman turned atheist, the greater majority of his native loyalists pursuing him in wholesale abandonment of the pews of the Christian church with greater followership than was accorded Moses in the flight from Egypt. But if the Omnipotent inspired the flight from Egypt, who inspired the flight of the English from the house of His Only Begotten Son?

Therein breathes the nerve-centre of this story, for, with the rule of Britannia still holding sway over much of the world (most especially the 'third' part of it), the Afro-Saxon is thrown into perplexity: first he is declared backward for perceived primitive pagan practices, and then, with the echo of his hosanna over his full conversion still ringing in the air, he is considered no less backward for his dogged retention of his Christian faith in what is fashionably chorused in the West as the "post-Christian era" by the very 'New World' Samaritans who 'civilized' him in Christ's holy name.

So why continue to celebrate Christmas? Let's ask the Englishman. Over to you, Oliver Wendell Holmes, for the foxy justification: "Most people are willing to take the Sermon on the Mount as a flag to sail under, but few will use it as a rudder by which to steer." Good advice, in the light of Christmas being the only time in the year when the English pretend to be human.

The 'Afro-Saxon' (or any other racial attachment of the Saxon status) will discover, at the end of the day, that there are actually sundry profits to be derived from such a posture, rather than it being an affliction. As the casual observer, he will discover more about the Englishman than the Englishman knows about himself (as is applicable to his own original countrymen – and to himself, as viewed from two vastly different perspectives),

The Englishman, really, is quite a remarkable specimen. It would be hard to imagine anyone else who could assert his independence to his Maker with the legitimate reason, "Lead me not into temptation: I can find the way myself."

Without prejudice to the truism that "An Englishman is a man who lives on an island in the North Sea, governed by Scotsmen" (Philip Guedella, essayist and historian), and that such a man is the principal character under study herein above all else, the 'Englishman' is also applied as a broad term to denote all local members of the Caucasian/Aryan group of humanity. Let us not lean too much on the word 'Caucasian', for even men of darker hue from whom the Englishman is said to have been extracted (most notably the Pakistanis) are themselves of Caucasian stock; and with the near-extinct practice of 'Paki-bashing' in London, the ethnic purity for which the Aryan/Europeans seek to monopolise that expression 'Caucasian' for their own exclusive identification may not be justified.

Be that as it may, in so far as it relates to this scheme of things, this past, current and futuristic review of the Englishman in his relationship with himself as arguably the 'first' in line of the racial groups, with the African as the third and 'last' in line, and with the Omnipotent as the long-suffering Maker of the insufferable *Homo sapiens*, sets out – in principle – to paint the Englishman in complimentary colours for the uniquely intriguing specimen that he is; and this should not be discounted by the fact that when the Englishman himself agrees to something "in principle", he means that he has not the slightest intention of carrying it out in practice. With that premise established, it remains to be seen from the pages ahead where the world is heading to with the Englishman in it.

CHAPTER 4

Echoes of 'the Infidel'

The most awesome character I ever met was a chap given the nickname 'the Infidel'. I was privileged to make his acquaintance in the closing pages of Eldridge Cleaver's 1969 soul-searching classic *Soul on Ice*, which Cleaver wrote as a convict in his prison cell. It explored the vexed themes of the struggle against subjugation by the black man in America, the myths and heroes of the white race, and interracial sexual congress.

The pages in question depict four aggrieved characters who are engaged in a choleric debate on the evil of colour prejudice, each having an axe to grind almost to the point of seeking faults in each other's physical appearance or mind-set as an escape route through which to vent their own individual pent-up frustrations. Notwithstanding the heap of indictments each of them built up against the crimes of the slave masters and their descendants, the Infidel made this angry declaration:

"There is no love left between a black man and a black woman. Take me, for instance. I love white women and hate black women... Ain't no such thing as an ugly white woman. A white woman is beautiful even if she's bald and has only one tooth... I love her skin, her soft smooth, white skin. I like to just lick her white skin as sweet, fresh honey flows from her pores, and just to touch her long, soft, silky hair. There's a softness about a white woman, something delicate and soft inside her... but a nigger bitch seems to be full of steel, granite-hard and resisting, not soft and submissive like a white woman. Ain't nothing more beautiful than a white woman's hair being blown by the wind. The white woman is more than a woman to me... She's like a goddess, a symbol. My love for her is religious and beyond fulfilment. I worship her. I love a white woman's dirty drawers...

"When I'm on a nigger bitch, I close my eyes and concentrate real hard, and pretty soon I get to believing that I'm riding one of them bucking blondes. I tell you the truth, that's the only way that I can bust my nuts with a black bitch, to close my eyes and pretend that she is Jezebel. If I was to look down and see a black bitch underneath me or if my hand happened to feel her nappy hair, that would be the end, it would be all over. I might as well get up and split because I wouldn't be able to get anything down, even if I piled her all night long. Any black man who says he don't dig Jezebel is a goddam liar. I believe that if a leader wanted to unite the Negroes in a solid unity, he could do so very easily. All he'd have to do is promise every black man a white woman and every black woman a white man. He would have so many followers that he wouldn't know what to do with them all."

The Infidel concludes his confession with an even more damning revelation: "There is a sickness in the whites that lies at the core of their madness, and this sickness makes them act in many different ways. But there is one way it makes some of them act that seems to contradict everything we know about whitey and shakes many blacks up when they first encounter it... there are white men who will pay you to fuck their wives."

Phew!

Having adopted a voracious appetite for current reading around the time that *Soul on Ice* was published in a global storm, I was startled by that last revelation, but was not unfamiliar with the concept of the worldwide perception of the superior feminine attributes of the Caucasian woman. This was tacitly recognised, but rarely voiced, by practically all men of varying hue, and there was surely a subterranean yearning from the darkest of them to sample and feast on that psychologically unobtainable goddess. The Infidel merely voiced an explosive truth that was suppressed in self-conscious silence by his fellows of midnight hue worldwide. I did allude to this same yearning in my earlier published works.

Even when taken out of context, the Infidel's last statement quoted above was startling enough on hitting the eye. The ears of the audience in his cell were no less riveted, and surely they listened for an elaboration both for invaluable education and for the enhancement of learning. Likewise there is the need to reproduce additional data that they heard... "You go with him, and he drives you to their home. The three of you go into the bedroom. There is a certain type who will leave you and his wife alone and tell you to pile her real good. After it is all over, he will pay you and drive you to wherever you want to go. Then there are some who like to peep at you through a keyhole and watch you have his woman, or peep at you through a window, or lie under the bed and listen to the creaking of the bed as you work out. There is another type who likes to masturbate while he stands beside the bed and watches you pile her. There is the type who likes to eat his woman up after you get through piling her. And there is the type who only wants you to pile her for a while, just long enough to thaw her out and kick her motor over and arouse her to heart, then he wants you to jump off real quick and he will jump onto her and together they can make it from there by themselves."

This author did not wholly agree with the Infidel in the way he viewed the foregoing alternatives in the taking of pleasure. The choice of bedroom frolics could not be labelled a "madness" because it belongs to the pigeon-hole of culture, and no universal means exists for measuring cultures. What may be good for the European goose may not necessarily be good for the African gander. Otherwise colour prejudice and racism would not exist.

While the European may find himself alone in this exclusive 'ultra-modern' advancement in amplifying the pleasures of the flesh, every man of midnight hue will vow to the highest point of Heaven that his better half has never been – and can never be – compromised in the aforesaid manner. India's lucrative tea and curry industries are not spiced with such a menu, and the very best of Chinese sweet and sour would turn decidedly bitter at the mere scent of such a recipe. But if the opportunity appeared, by chance, to be on offer under a cloak of secrecy, it is not easy to draw an inference that any randy male, of any race, of any colour, would decline the compelling temptation of such a novelty in the name of experience or adventure.

Between the European and the rest of the world, the varying attitudes on the matter are not dissimilar to the discrepancies between capitalism and communism. Their essential difference, in the view of Phelps Adams, is this: "The communist, seeing the rich man and his fine home, says: 'No man should have so much.' The capitalist, seeing the same thing, says: 'All men should have as much." Likewise, as The Infidel criticises some features of the Caucasian's bedroom frolics as "madness", the European will tell him that all men should be unashamed to enjoy free, imaginative love as it pleases them.

After my own encounter with the 'Infidel', I was wont to wonder if the African-American ought not to feel some measure of appreciation for this magnanimity and view it in the light of token compensation for the 400 years of slavery they endured. Some of them had even been treading the wrong path in their pursuit of a 'Black Muslim' faith as a way of rebellion against the supposedly white Christian God of their oppressors. Go back to Christ and apologise at once, I thought. There you are – after all those years of subjugation, the wind of remorse from the camp of your oppressors blew away the permissive relief that gave you the go-ahead to copulate with every shade, shape and size of female Aryan whiteness, screwing even into the royal bedrooms of Europe and the Americas.

Compare that to the policies enacted by the Arab slave trade of the Black African, when the practice was to castrate every slave to prevent the 'unthinkable' idea of copulation between the Black African male and the Arab woman. One can almost count the number of marriages between an African male and an Arab female on the fingers of one hand. How often do you see that happening? And those Arab chaps are the hardcore adherents to the Moslem faith that you now want to adopt. Yet look at the new fashion, the new craze, of black-white copulation on both sides of the Atlantic: how better is racial equality exemplified by this early period of change?

Robert H. Decoy, your postulation in *The Nigger Bible* is misplaced when you proclaim: "When standing to be judged and condemned... before the benches and bars in the courts of their Mosaic Laws, then remember, my son, to reach down and cover, hold on to your testicles, for when all else is lost, here hangs your last semblance of Power. To protect them is your spiritual salvation."

Come now, M'sieur Decoy, save all that humbug for the former

Arab traders in Black African slaves, not the merciful justice of the English courts. Leave the loving, creative Englishman alone. Try to consider the Englishman's case as postulated by Karl Jung: "Without this playing with fantasy, no creative work has ever yet come to birth. The debt we owe to the play of imagination is incalculable." "You're telling me!" I exclaim. Imagination is the basis of the Englishman's total liberation from the cell of ignorance, complex and inhibition. He acts out his forbidden fantasies, and damns what society thinks. He gets more and more people to see his line of reasoning, and presently there seems to be created the basis for a peaceful society, a peaceful world, *without* the Prince of Peace (that is, our Lord and Saviour).

Next there follows a holy war which he mounts against the 'unholiness' of Christian repression that threatens such 'deviancy' with hell-fire. Does it really require George Bernard Shaw to remind us: "As long as more people will pay admission to a theatre to see a naked body than to see a naked brain, the drama will languish"? The Englishman will add to this: "The world has already seen the products of our naked brains." They are inherent in the wonders of science and technology. Hence these wonders represent, in turn, the legitimate licence to explore and enhance the pleasures of the flesh as the 'higher' animals that the English are, the 'higher' animals that made these wonders, and to break down all laid-down barriers of convention and prejudice which militate against self-improvement in the eyes of a free self and giving 'our all' in other spheres of human progress. With a free mind, there is then created the basis, the clear unencumbered path, to forge ahead with human advancement.

"So, Great Architect of the Universe," declares the Englishman, "please allow us to apply the franchise of free will which You bestowed upon us in the way and manner that we see fit, and forbid us not – for ours is the Kingdom of Earth, the land of flesh, so that we may be permitted to make the best of fleshly needs from which we derive pleasure."

The divine silence and the raising of divine hands in a tacit act of surrender to the will of man represent an eloquent way of saying, "So be it. Fornicate in haste, repent at leisure."

So the Englishman will no longer be driven out of Eden, like Adam and Eve, or have London and San Francisco destroyed like Sodom and Gomorrah. In good time, in the wake of his practising his elected pleasures of the flesh, the improbable Aids epidemic visited mankind, spreading like global cancer as Britannia ruled the sperm-waves.

The beauty about the Englishman, as the Pied Piper of Mother Earth (which includes Hamlyn), is his evident satisfaction, his supreme but quiet confidence, over the idea that his 200-plus years of industrial experience – ushered in by the Industrial Revolution – have effectively entrenched in his civilisation the equivalent of heaven on earth. From his exalted posture as the Soul of Reason, secured by iron pillars of scientific logic and creative flair as his own self-made 'divine' sanctuary from which to referee every facet of the game of life all over the globe (in subtle manipulation of those in power), the Englishman has secured a 'tacit' licence to entertain and practise even the 'unorthodox' and 'unconventional' in the name of research and creativity. What essentially constitutes the 'unorthodox' and 'unconventional'? It is a breakaway from encumbrances of traditional custom to secure freedom in one's ways, rooted in the conviction that if one follows reason far enough, invariably it leads one to conclusions that are contrary to reason.

At the end of the day, the set of rules enshrined in the original book of convention, the Holy Bible, has been gradually marginalised by that art of going wrong with confidence – logic. Man has instituted his opposition, Science, to ask questions which, when no plausible answer is forthcoming, create a new set of rules that cater for and justify the unconventional in the name of freedom. Finding nothing remotely wrong with pork after detailed scientific experiment, for instance, the biblical injunction against its consumption is poohpoohed in favour of the succulence of pork chops. Likewise snail waters the mouth with the specially-prepared delicacy of *escargot*; while the legs of the venomous frog have become an unforgettable eating experience.

Seen in this vein, the commodity behind the greatest intensity of physical pleasure questions the conventional morale that its indulgence must be confined to the institution of wedded bliss, and not before or outside it. Even then, if it is indeed true that "in sin did my mother conceive me", that instrument for bolstering a prejudice – logic, challenges, "What harm does it cause if the same conception is achieved prior to wedded bliss? In such instances, are the sensations involved in the process less fulfilling? Is such a sin harmful because it is forbidden, or is it forbidden because it is harmful? Where exactly is the intrinsic harm to be felt in the course of execution?"

As confusion sets in with the various apparent contradictions attending the issue, it seems only inevitable that, as Bishop Fulton J. Sheen observes: "Sex has become one of the most discussed subjects of modern times. The Victorians pretended it did not exist; the moderns pretend that nothing else exists." No less inevitably, scientific analysis has sought to cloak the commodity with a garb of respectability with the argument, as postulated by Eddie Cantor, "Lust isn't all there is to sex. Sex isn't all there is to love. But love is almost all there is to life... Love isn't like a reservoir – you'll never drain it dry... love/live. Switch a single letter and they're just the same." But John Ciardi is more specific, perhaps more realistic, as regards the different manifestations of this commodity: "Love is the word used to label the sexual excitement of the young, the habituation of the middle-aged, and the mutual dependence of the old."

Still, among the moderns there is the initial magnetic thread of sexuality, linking up all the 'uniform' points of the love game. Such sexuality is honed to a fine art by the unparalleled genius of the Englishman's creative flair. To facilitate and expedite that elusive dream, all prejudice against aspects of personal behaviour which can be deemed to be perfectly natural and constitute no harm to any third party must be removed. So let every man bugger and sodomise to his heart's desire as long as all participating minds are willing. Christian repression, then, has come under siege as the Englishman goes all out to enforce the law that there is no reason why the unthinkable should not become not only the thinkable, but the do-able. As Herbert Hoover said: "Words without actions are the assassins of idealism." This was hailed by Thomas Huxley – "Science is simply common sense at its best – that is, rigidly accurate in observation, and merciless to fallacy in logic", and divined by the logic of John Dewey – "Every great advance in science has issued from a new audacity of imagination".

So it was that the Murrays' patriotic English policy of continuous improvement somewhat revised the irrational prejudices of husband Frank against non-white people (most notably the black man) in favour of the more benign tolerance of wife Anne (not their real names). The beneficiary of their accommodating hospitality was Sam, a dusky indigene from somewhere south of the Sahara whose prowess on the tennis and squash courts, and in dance, was matched with a quick wit, keen intelligence, and articulate, down-to-earth congeniality that collectively endeared him to Frank Murray of all people. Frank's new-found

'romance' with a Black person was hailed and encouraged by Anne as a whole new world of initiation, and before long the three developed a close companionship that served as a tribute to the value of social intercourse and human relations.

Now Frank and Anne Murray were not your run-of-the-mill English couple. Both had sprung from the middle bracket of the English class ladder, bred from preparatory, public and finishing schools of note, and made their hard-earned livelihood in respectable disciplines. In their late twenties, they were in no haste to start a family, and made the best use of the available time in early marriage to enjoy themselves as a couple. Wedded bliss usually catered for a contrast in looks, either 'beauty' with the 'beast', and rarely two 'beasts' or two 'beauties'. Frank and Anne were a striking pair of beauties, both blonde, with Anne's perfect features bedecked with a generous sprinkling of delicious freckles. Against Frank's tall, angular appearance, Anne was a big woman, of fair height and bosomy physique. Both were basically cheerful and extrovert, with Anne exhibiting more of a quiet English reserve, while Frank was adventurous, an inveterate alcoholic, and was often coarse in his application of humour.

In spite of the wide circle of friends that the couple enjoyed, they treasured their privacy, and revelled in the 'forbidden' pleasures of pornographic 'art'. They went a step further by acting out some of the fantasies with each other, a development initiated by Frank's spirit of adventure and daring. Anne was mildly amused to start with, participating on the strength of matrimonial 'obligations', as it were, but she was gradually converted. While Anne allowed herself to be 'corrupted' only by the seemingly impenetrable privacy provided by their matrimonial 'oneness', together with the 'feeling is believing' truism of variety as being indeed life's principal spice, she was able to jokingly dismiss Frank's confessions of occasional titillating fantasies of seeing her in adulterous perverse copulation with other lovers. Frank seemed a perfect candidate for Oscar Wilde's thesis that "Imagination is a quality given a man to compensate him for what he is not, and a sense of humour was provided to console him for what he is."

For Anne her husband's confessed fantasies were beyond the realms of possibility in real life. In fact they were unthinkable – that is, until Frank brought Sam, a young black man, into their bedroom frolics. Time led to friendship with Sam, and Frank encouraged him and Anne to take dance lessons. The physical closeness between Sam and Anne that resulted left Frank wanting more. What had previously been unthinkable happened after a drinking spree at a local pub that went on till closing time, when Sam escorted his friends back home for more booze and food. Later the mood of fun 'under the influence' appeared to take on a more carefree, playful pitch. Amid scenes of seemingly innocuous taunts and insults between husband and wife, Frank bullied her into their bedroom, beckoned Sam to follow, and tied her hands to the bedposts.

Relating the event to this author years later as a divorcée, Anne would recall that scene as some unbelievable slow-motion dream in which, in spite of herself, she was a willing participant in all that took place. She would recall herself saying, "Don't be silly, Frank, untie me at once", and found it undignified to offer even token physical resistance. But Frank proceeded to undress her, slowly, stage by stage, item by item, after which he waved a command to Sam to go ahead and have his fill. Sam obliged, albeit hesitantly to start with, and Anne found herself responding to his love-making with a suppressed frenzy and heat of passion that she had never felt before. Frank played with himself, spurred on by the excitement of real-life spectatorship of the unthinkable being a reality, and climaxed at the same time as the mating duo on the bed.

At the end of the exercise, Anne ordered her husband sharply to untie her, and then gathered her clothes and stomped out of the bedroom, saying, "You will never get me to do *that* again!"

For Anne and Frank, there was a swamp of guilt to wade through afterwards, and that was the end of their precious friendship with Sam, whose eyes they could never look into again. But where was the sacredness of their marriage thereafter? Ironically, in due course it appeared to be strengthened by that first outlandish experiment with planned adultery. Ultimately they took to the practice like fish to water, developing a select wife-swapping circle of English friends who held fast to the conviction that exchanging partners was an effective palliative against possessiveness and jealousy, and was in line with the divine principle of sharing.

I had to chance upon Gay Talese's *Thy Neighbour's Wife* to appreciate the universal scale of this supremely English rebellion against the divine prohibition of adultery. Be blessed, dear Robert H. Decoy for your educative treatise in *The Nigger Bible*, where we learn in Verse 7 that "There are but three requirements... for a Nigger who wishes to become a well-adjusted and acceptable "Negro", three modern Caucasian sophistications: (1) Abide homosexuality as a form of culture. (2) Develop a marked toleration for the practice of swapping wives. (3) Embrace the custom of eating pussy.

CHAPTER 5

The two faces of bestiality

The Englishman has come a long way since his emergence as a savage from ice-age caves through servitude to his Roman conquerors to the glory of empire under the forward thrust of Queen Victoria's imperial finger ordering the invasion and plundering of distant lands. In fact, the Englishman has since changed almost beyond recognition, beyond belief, since those glorious days when he ruled half the world. The sugar coating that comprises his unique demonstration of charm and refinement, dignifying his supremacy in applying the fine art of logic and deduction, unhappily fails to conceal his predilection for sin for very long.

Having plundered and colonized half the world, the spoils of conquest elevated the Englishman to its greatest seat of power. Pitchforked as he has been from the savagery of cave-man existence (when he had almost frozen to death) to the pinnacle of power, glory and comfort, there had been little time for spirituality. In as much as a principal feature of his refining touch comprised a whole-hearted appreciation of Christian dogma to start with, it did not occur to the Englishman that it was probably for that very reason that he found favour in the sight of the Ancient of Days and was specially rewarded with his unique larger-than-life rise to glory against all conceivable odds.

There he was, with no significant resource other than cheap coal that provided blazing warmth from the deathly cold, saddled with a generally disagreeable climate, on a meaningless dot of an island, and with a capital city barely one square mile in size (and yet the utopian rendezvous of world tourism, world politics, and entrepreneurial inspiration), yet he emerged the most advanced and organized specimen of the most advanced species on the globe. Here indeed was the accomplished English puppet-master making rulers all over the world dance to his tune by bringing the riches from their colonized soils to merry old England.

Significant aspects of that 'merriment' are enshrined in the enviable etiquette peculiar to the Englishman. For instance, note the manner in which he sits up at the dining table with a slight protrusion of his arse (never mind that it looks comically coarse, especially in the case of a big-arsed lady), and watch the way he deftly packs food with his knife on to the back of his fork, turns his head a little to the side as he guides the food into his mouth with practised grace, and then munches evenly with his mouth closed. Observe the melting warmth with which our English gentleman will ask an alien newcomer, "How are you? Are you well?" If this warmth is misread for more than the basic civil communication that it is intended to be, and he is regaled in response with a detailed description of the visitor's stomach problems and the consequent bouts of diarrhoea to which he is being subjected, the gentlemanly posture will undergo a marked deterioration. He will take pains to explain: "You will find that here in England, unpleasant as I'm sure they must be, the workings of your inner anatomy are not as a rule of any interest to an English audience and should not ordinarily be brought up for mention." Chapter closed.

The Englishman is a maestro in the economical use of good words. He will not usually talk with his mouth full. When he feels tempted to throw in a word in contribution to the flow of talk in between mouthfuls, or in any other gathering of good people, he will maintain a keen regard for *sensible* talk. He will flutter his eyes discreetly to enhance the appearance of humility, and purse his lips to accord with each pleasing inflection in a show of elegant diction. As a rule he will endeavour to wait to be asked for his opinion rather than make an arbitrary contribution. He is always ready to apologise even for having been created – for every petty little fault he might display, like accidentally bumping into someone, or failing to observe the "Ladies first" tradition, or for interrupting, or for not measuring up in one way or the other.

But the Englishman is an avowed critic of anyone else who fails generally to measure up to his standards, albeit couched in a tone of disarming diplomacy. (Diplomacy is to say the nastiest things in the nicest way, remember?) In addition, the fault-seeking eyes of the Englishman will miss *nothing*, not the slightest speck of dust on the alien's shirt-collar, or a missing button on your coat, not poor physical appearance, not insufficient humility or decorum, not bad English, not failure to talk sense (or to talk out of turn), nor a lack of purposeful gait, or idleness that would signify – as nothing else can – an inability to contribute to the upkeep of Her Majesty's Government. The Englishman's looks and impressions can kill in his indefatigable search for the perfection that eludes him. These cultural niceties serve to enrich the unique flavour of merry old England. At the end of the day, it would almost appear that the Lord Jesus had declared the appointment of him and his fellow islanders as his chosen people. If the Englishman is arguably rivalled by his other European counterparts in Christian refinement, without a doubt he emerges as the first amongst equals.

His early infatuation with Christ is touchingly reflected in his aesthetic disposition, which is second nature. His hymns and songs of praise bear this out, suggesting to the stranger that much of the time the Englishman's keen senses are scanning the skies to see God's handiwork emblazoned across the heavens. His hymns and songs take in all the wonders of nature, from the dizzying effects of a miraculous sunset to breath-taking landscapes, to the rich diversity of wildlife engaged in its peculiar activities of survival to lingering winds that soothe nature to sleep, and to stars that tremble through ether. His descriptions are presented in rich, vivid colours, expressed with a positive relish for dialogue that benefits greatly from that greatest medium of expression – the English language.

In such instances even the Englishman's cultural disposition to silence seems to be infringed, and he is wont to exclaim, with a practised economy of words, "Isn't it gorgeous!" His poetic mind is inspired with pensive tenderness by the magic of nature, gradually elevated to sublime contemplation, ultimately motivated to visualize the existence of art in every creation – including sin. Accordingly he has refined sin, cloaking it with such beautifully-tailored robes that patrons of free love promote healthy debate on the subject: Pornography – Sin or Art?

So it was that the 1960s swept in something called *change*. It was personified by such celebrated heroines as Christian Keeler, Xaviera Hollander and Mandy Rice-Davies, to name but three. These doyens of erotic art demonstrated unparalleled proficiency in the spicing of bedroom frolics. As a result the unbelievable happened, and the world stared open-mouthed as eminent figures in British political life were bowled over like skittles in the ensuing hair-raising kiss-and-tell-all scandals. Christine Keeler even brought down the Conservative Government of Sir Harold Macmillan. Thenceforth something akin to re-enactments of Original Sin and Sodom and Gomorrah became the order of the day in high society life, and England, personified by the Englishman, changed beyond recognition. He was now transformed into some rebellious Pied Piper of Hamlyn, now *mis*leading the world as he played erotic tunes on the flute and strayed from the path of Christian civilization.

The greatest dancer of these erotic tunes was Mariella Novotny. By the time I was privileged to make her acquaintance, and later become her friend, he had conferred on the Infidel the accolade, "Like Macbeth, thou shalt be King hereafter". For most of his postulations on inter-colour congress in the game of Eros could not be faulted.

The said Mariella Novotny (now of blessed memory) was a sophisticated beauty with breasts crafted in heaven, except that they wielded an earthbound voluptuousness. She should, by rights, be graced with the camouflage of a pseudonym to sanctify the laws of privacy. But in the role of a modern Joan of Arc, she initiated, with her natural identity, a war against the incarceration of bedroom frolics behind closed doors. As the unabashed mother of Europe's 'Permissive Society', with a 'kiss-and-tell-all' policy of personal research – in practical terms – of other unexplored avenues to the enhancement of ecstasy, she was dubbed by the British press "The Most Shocking Girl In The World". The daughter of an 'Iron Curtain' statesman who was a cousin of the former President Novotny of Czechoslovakia, she married into the top echelons of English society, wedding eccentric antiques dealer Hod Dibben, who, on his own well-publicised admission, was blessed from childhood with a total absence of jealousy. This was developed in marital life with a passion for spying on Mariella in a variety of compromising positions with male partners.

Mariella was a tall, well-endowed woman with sharp, staring eyes which were encircled by sooty radials of mascara and elongated false lashes. This appearance was enhanced by a full-lipped pout (the voluptuary's badge) and a strawberry-blonde fringe of hair that fell in graceful waves to her shoulders, framing an exquisite, delicate oval face.

Mariella became more English than the English, both in diction and in marriage. She befriended many of the world's most powerful men – and women (the latter with lesbian gratification). They included tycoons, politicians, international statesmen, film stars, musicians, industrial millionaires, and artists. Inevitably, she then became "Europe's most provocative author" with her scorching first novel *King's Road*, which exposed un-aristocratic goings-on in the bedrooms of the elite on both sides of the Atlantic. *King's Road* was published one month before Yours Truly's *Nigger at Eton* by good old Leslie Frewin, who laughed all the way to the bank with Mariella's novel. With sales made to 10 countries in almost as many languages, Frewin disclosed to Yours Truly, shaking his head for emphasis, "Miss Novotny did terribly well with her first book. That's probably her trouble – she did *too* well. I've just sent her another large cheque."

But Frewin saw red when he learnt that Yours Truly had become well acquainted with Mariella, giving the reason, "I really don't approve of associations between authors. You tend to lose authors that way."

At the age of only 17, the inimitable Mariella Novotny threw incredible society parties with a menu complete with a full-plumed peacock and dressed badger. Included in the evening's entertainment was a naked 'Man-in-the Mask', which resulted in a controversy which became the subject of an official Government inquiry by Law Lord Denning. Playing to the world public gallery and with a drama-packed life that exuded sexual aristocracy, Mariella waltzed from one stage of trouble to the other. First she was arrested by the FBI in America as a "wayward minor", then she was unwittingly involved in the Christine Keeler–Stephen Ward–Ivanov sex-cum-spy scandal that brought down Macmillan's government.

With the passage of years, the weight of motherhood, and the stress of matrimonial duties collectively applying the brakes against over-consumption of everything that life and flesh had to offer, Mariella became the highest paid columnist for the 'X-rated mass-circulation magazine *CLUB International*, providing graphic details of a career charged with the larger-than-life adventures of an inveterate 'nympho'. One example was her generous indulgence, arranged with her West Indian black lover, in gratifying 200 black youths one after the other. It was Mariella's belief that she had performed an essential social service towards racial harmony by fulfilling the dreams of some men of midnight hue who yearned to score with seemingly unobtainable white Madonnas.

"I was just curious," she confessed to me, setting her sight on indigenes south of the Sahara as the next set of beneficiaries. Heavens above, Mariella, you have devoured 200 of London's most virile black youths, and now you want to follow them up with Africa's most abundant resource – manpower? Oh yes, she insisted. Moreover, from the realm of African occult magic – potions, trances, spells, etc – could there be extracted a new dimension of outlandish, nerve-stretching sensation to enhance the pleasure of the mating game?

One could not help but admire Hod Dibben, her exemplary

middle-aged husband, eccentric with his pony-tail hair-style, tubby physique and poker-face but in every consideration the accomplished English host whose overall air of upper-class respectability belied his peeping-tom activities. He demonstrated culinary flair by the preparation of splendid English roast joints, roast potatoes and gravy to entertain a guest who had been cavorting with his wife in her private room up in the attic of this rustic cottage in the country wilds of Colchester. There, with whips, suspender belts and other implements of perversion, a rich variety of the dramatic frolics of Marquis de Sade prevailed on the bed with her male partners, who would beat her nakedness in a burlesque drama before the final copulation. From some hidden peep-hole, Hod Dibben would take in the drama with covert relish. Back in Africa, if the 'interloper' were to sit to lunch with the wayward wife, daughter and knowing husband, without a doubt it would be his spirit consuming his own beheaded flesh. But trust the English gentleman to make his guest feel a part of the family with the inimitable hospitality for which the English have become so well known.

And after the three-course meal, the return to the 'basics' upstairs is preceded by a sudden thought by the irrepressible adventuress, who says to her little daughter Gillian, "Listen, I want you to watch this."

"You're not taking Gillian with you?" hubby Hod queries in subtle but unmistakable disapproval.

"Oh, okay, on second thoughts, better not."

Later, Mariella is anaesthetized by passion after reaching further great heights of wild abandon. She provokes a thousand thoughts on the Englishman's obsession for endless 'practical' research into this area of human weakness. It had become like a drug, an addiction, a spell which, having already accorded man knowledge possessed by 'gods', continued to beckon in encouragement of further exploration, with a tacit, tantalizing promise of greater mind-blowing ecstasy that would usher in unbelievable secrets of Divinity.

For the Englishman, personified by Mariella, the mating game had been transformed from a weakness into superhuman strength that had, sequentially, turned sane pleasure into distracted obsession – refined by the very fact of its having burst open the closet that had been incarcerating it for the freedom and fresh air of public display and acceptability. In the wake of her mad ecstasy, her breasts are the size and shape of tennis balls, and are now as hard as concrete, their red nipples extended in wanton invitation – secreting, as if by a miracle, a milk-like fluid. "By God, how the hell do you do that?" one wants to know. "TT Milk, I bet."

There comes a faint droopy-eyed smile.

"By the way, what's with the decision not to bring Gillian to see the show?" one further wants to know.

"Well, she's still a little child, you know, and it wouldn't be right for her to see her mother naked with a stranger."

"Who told you that you were naked?" an outraged divine voice interrupts with the rage of thunder from the Pearly Gates above. "Have you been eating that adulterous fruit which I ordered you not to eat?"

"The Western scientist cuckolded me, o Lord," says Mariella in despair. "He said there was nothing intrinsically or morally wrong with putting repressed natural desires into practical application among people of like mind and feelings."

To the Western scientist: "What is this you have done? You have diffused theoretical and practical atheism on a worldwide scale and led mankind in rebellion against my laws. Through the medium of social communication you have extolled sin that I designed exclusively for the beasts of the field as a positive value and good for its practice by men. Because you have done this, I shall smite Western civilization with decadence, and I shall swallow it up at Armageddon."

The African participant beats a hasty retreat from the unwholesome scenario, seeking new pastures in the diseased pleasures of sin to which he has been jinxed by this helpless addiction to the drug of white womanhood – barely mindful of the fact that its spell-binding effects on a frenzied African suitor, who now wishes to taste nothing else, are causing him to stray further away from the earlier disciplinary teachings of Christ...

An observer in some fourth dimension whose interest might have been accidentally captured by the foregoing events would, at this point, have swung his long lens away from the Colchester residence of the Dibbens to focus some fourteen years into the future, on a developing artificial city south of the Sahara. There, observing the author in a scene of crisis in his original home environment, he would have been compassionately horrified by the cultural tightrope separating purgatory from hell which Yours Truly would be compelled to attempt to walk in consequence of having been immersed in a refining society that laid emphasis on the pleasures of the flesh as an important consideration, as an acid test, for meaningful *social* intercourse.

This author stands anonymous in the midst of a crowd of sadistic human moths drawn by the light of trouble to feast their senses on the charred remains of a lynched criminal who had been caught in flight, stoned into oblivion, drenched with petrol and then set alight, a disused car-tyre pulled tightly over his body to keep the flames of death burning for as long as possible. Amidst other jeers and scathing commentary, a female teenager giggles derisively to her mate, "Heh, heh, look at this shit." Our conjectured observer, some advanced English being of the finest breed, grimaces and recoils from the gory sight, condemning the jungle justice in the strongest terms. Yours Truly, in patriotic defence of his people and culture, points out that the punishment was commensurate with the gravity of the crime.

"No crime under God's canopy calls for such barbaric reprisal," contends our observer.

"Hear what he did then: he stole a day-old baby, placed it alive in a mortar, and proceeded to pound it with a pestle until it was mashed into thick paste, which would later be smeared over the body as a magic potion that will expedite and enhance the money-making process."

The face of our observer falls apart, and he seems ready to gag.

"Yes, exactly," say I. "So you see, that punishment was perfectly in order. Even you would have wished to give him the Chinese death of a thousand cuts. Never apportion sympathy and condemnation based on mere *prima facie* evidence of cruelty until you *hear* what the victim did."

Having apparently decided he had heard enough, our observer begins to take his leave, shaking his head, and saying, "God left Africa a long time ago" before vanishing into the fourth dimension.

"Hey come back, don't say that," calls Yours Truly. Our observer pops his head out from the fourth dimension. "God never destroyed the twin cities of Sodom and Gomorrah for the crime of barbaric violence against ritual killers of babies," I continue. "He took that punitive action against sexual deviancy, such as is today practised in the Western world with great relish and ritual. We simply have a case of two faces of bestiality, respectively valued by the different people who practise them. To you we are worse than animals due to our penchant for seemingly barbaric punishment; no less are the sexual varieties of modern Europe like a tribute to animal values and possible psychiatric imbalance."

"I would rather watch the sex life of Europeans than all that," counters our observer.

So be it, O Worshipful Master of the Voyeuristic Art. Back then to England.

CHAPTER 6

Midnight redemption

In England the lawyers for Mariella Novotny, acting on instructions from her agent, drew up a preliminary agreement which inserted a prohibitive knot in every clause that only a party to it who had left his brain at home would have failed to grasp. The long and short of everything was that Mariella's agent dreaded the thought of the whole project – doubtless nursing an image of Africa not unrelated to the first insight availed by our conjectured observer. They did not find the need to let 'innocent-minded' Mariella know all that.

Leslie Frewin, to whom Yours Truly gave sight of the proposed agreement, was even more outraged that his ultra-respectable list of honourable titles could be discoloured by the unpalatable recipe of sex potions from Africa. Moreover he was none too happy to grasp that the relationship between his two 'errant' authors had attained a level of familiarity that surpassed mere acquaintanceship. He delivered himself of only ten words, but they clearly summarised the dimness of his views on the whole matter: "If you sign that contract, you are lumbered for life."

At the end of the day Mariella's agent was happy, and Leslie Frewin was happy, when the whole deal fell apart and was relegated to the dustbin. Mariella was peeved. I merely shrugged and pursued my adventurous life with my head held relatively high, confident in the security of steady income from freelance journalism, as a book critic, and employment as a managing editor of a hardback book publishing outfit that was gaining ground with titles which were attracting favourable reviews and impressive sales.

On the social scene, there was the high-life and low-life of Britain's turned-on beautiful people availed by London, that global headquarters of utopian refinement, where the rule of law flourished triumphant and eternal peace created a bed of roses for everyone of peaceful disposition, where you luxuriated in the spick-and-span castle that was the Englishman's home, where you wiped your mouth after generous indulgence in succulent chops at lavish cocktail parties, and wiped your mouth again after further indulgence without injury to your stomach, and then flirted with those dainty English angel(a)s; where you thrilled to the blood-boiling adventure of illicit love across the colour line.

By the first quarter of the 1980s I had reached saturation point with this routine of 'love-and-be-damned' and set my sights homeward for a final withdrawal from England after 22 years. Reviewing the latter part of those years, what had settled was the dust of empty futility rather than fulfilment from bedroom relationships between black and white partners. The love-game was compartmented in the unedifying pigeon-hole of body and words, bereft of the human touch.

From the bedroom of aided-and-abetted adultery by both partners of the marital union, we move on to the fashion of basic promiscuity – no less perfected into a fine art by the relentless scrutiny of logic. In the same spirit of group copulation which finally gave tacit licence to the wife-swapping phenomenon, its scandalous touch tickled the fancy of even the courts as judges of alleged obscenity cases took off their spectacles and roared with laughter over witnesses' accounts of heaving white buttocks in the throes of group orgies.

Invariably it was white buttocks and the entwinement of white male and female limbs that made the headlines. Members of the non-white communities, who had forever complained of being left out of the scheme of things in the social order, must have heaved sighs of relief to have been excluded from the limelight. Colour prejudice, in this case, proved to be a blessing. The infamous nymphomaniac Christine Keeler, whose strict regard for truth caused the downfall of her lover, War Minister John Profumo, in June 1963, and the subsequent collapse of British Prime Minister Harold Macmillan's Conservative government, described these high society group orgies in a book.

Such liberated deviancy could not have been complete without its outlandish fringes to lend more spice to the quaintness of the imaginative flair that went into their creation. They served to reflect the point at which the 'kinky' desire for some form of more bizarre alternatives in erotic fulfilment hovered between sanity and extremism. Could one beat the experience of that delicious 'Dutch cheese' Xaviera Hollander, of *The Happy Hooker* fame, one of whose High Society English male clients was so driven by infatuation for his mistress that he "...will literally eat your shit from a spoon"? Check out *The Happy Hooker* for more such recipes.

Outside the compulsion of gainful employment, my priorities were generously devoted to the fun of flirtatious English social life, with particular emphasis on the intoxicating effects of the pleasures of English female flesh. The 'exclusive' beauty of quality English life was indivisibly interlocked with this aspect of its overall eccentricity, without which all the meat would be taken out of the English stew.

But there was an endearing colour that, for Yours Truly, gave this stew a unique flavour which was no less superbly English, like the middle-aged chap at Hatchard's bookshop in the city whose face bore a stern masculinity, while the rest of his body was garbed in the highest quality lady's wear, with a thigh-length blouse and black high-heels. The effect was completed by drooping ear-rings, red lipstick, rouged cheeks, eye-shadow, and auburn hair drawn back into a pony-tail. This refined transvestite seemed natural and composed, at home at the counter in dedicated attendance, communicating with customers in a rich English voice that sounded like a mixture of male bass and female contralto. Such a European novelty in an African setting would have attracted a sizeable crowd of ogle-eyed onlookers, bemused, bewildered, punctuating the air with exclamations of shock, mocking, unable to determine the kind of specimen presented before their eyes. No one of their kind could personalise such an oddity without being stoned to death for sacrilege. But here in England, with a culture that provided for the strict minding of one's own business, those chancing across this member of staff did just that and scarcely batted an eyelid.

No less touching was another unconventional character with a strikingly stout frame, attired with a woman's cap that somehow matched an outsized head, and coarse features as grey as paving stones. He had no real reason for joining me on my bench in Hyde Park as I idly watched the summer throng of sightseers saunter along Broad Walk. That eccentric specimen would have been stoned by an outraged mob had he been an African in Africa. Distracted, disgusted, Yours Truly heard himself blurt out, "Don't you feel a bit of a fool?" in contravention of the tradition to do as the English do and mind one's own business. The man's only response to Yours Truly's unguarded provocation was to sharply turn his head and look ahead, face lifted, lips tight in the traditional stiff-upper-lip attitude.

I was confident of being able to outrun the man should he lunge, and was tempted to persist. In a veiled effort at communication, I asked: "Can I buy you an ice-cream?"

In a poorly disguised male voice of impeccable aristocratic origins, he replied, "Look, young man, you mustn't be selfish now. You should ask yourself – 'am I being fair to this lady? Am I interfering with the privacy of this lady? Does this lady want to be left alone?'"

At this challenge, I remembered the counsel of John Barrymore: "The best way to fight a woman is with your hat. Grab it and run." I heeded it, and fled.

Having regard to other more outlandish features of this deviancy, the details of which would best be omitted from these pages, Yours Truly is wont to regard the aforesaid exclusion of his fellow black people in terms of some kind of 'midnight redemption'. Since the colour of the African's skin has remained the principal focus of attention for his dehumanisation by the other racial groups of the world, its indivisible kinship with midnight remains effectively impenetrable from any identification with the deviancy under reference.

Still, the Englishman's promotion of free love in all its supposedly rich and fulfilling varieties as a panacea for global peace and co-existence – in contrast with the reticence and conservatism that had hitherto characterized the cultures of the other racial groups – was effectively gaining ground in the corruption of a world beleaguered by conflict and 'repressive' Christian dogma. This was a world order headed by Western civilisation and accordingly, Western values held sway even if they attracted the raising of a brief eyebrow from other racial groups still enmeshed in the painful throes of transition.

Be that as it may, the success of the Englishman's indefatigable efforts to sell sexual freedom to an uninformed and impressionable global followership has been enhanced by the aesthetic beauty that is imbued in that greatest of all media of expression – the English language. This 'heavenly' commodity has woven its own special magic wand in the perceived glory of romantic love as it involved the European woman, who, for so many African males who have been 'privileged' to live in London since the end of the British Empire, presented a symbol of freedom, a sample of heaven. The European woman looked the part – a dainty little white lamb with exquisite diction, soft skin and long silk hair which, when caught in the breeze of poetry, flew behind her like the mane of a galloping mare. The European woman became the dream of almost every Europe-based African male. Physical involvement with her became like a drug, distorting reality, almost like a migraine that blotted out reason – if precisely because of her submissive nature, the ease of her availability, the near-demented violence of her response to copulation, and the voracity of her hunger for fulfilment, experiment and variety.

For the African male in London, desire for the white woman was certainly a triumph of imagination over intelligence. Her liberated sexuality compared unfavourably with the cultural reticence and resisting nature of African women back home. But what were the moral lessons to be learnt from this 'black market' promotion of the superstud myth of the black male and the 'unobtainability' of the white 'Madonna'? Where lay the hope of sealing any permanence in good race relations when the stakeholders were preoccupied in seeing each other as objects rather than human beings? Where was any hope of mutual respect? Did these myths not pander to the superficiality of white supremacist attitudes?

Prior to my final withdrawal from Britain's shores, I had made a couple of flying visits to my native Africa, where I recoiled at the horrific effects of the spirit of sexual freedom which had travelled across the airways to the niceties of what Erica Jong described in her novel *Fear of Flying* as "the zipless fuck". One had to take off one's hat in tribute to the monument of good salesmanship that the British had achieved in their subtle promotion of the erotic arts in the 'dark' continent. Truly the natives had divested themselves of their loin-cloths and graduated to knotting them around their necks and calling them ties, never to be called savages again.

But hark at the cost to the dignity of white womanhood. Poor you, English overlord. Once revered as the nearest visible creation to the Deity, your appearance in remote traditional villages used to put the indigenes to hysterical, helter-skelter flight, to peer from the safety of bushes at the alien 'white gods'. Folks of midnight hue would not dare to look you in the eye, and would grovel at the feet of your better half from the depths of subservience. The indigenes placed you on the pedestal, but you threw yourself down from it into the gutter when you elected to export sex magazines and movies for them to leer at, depicting your hitherto hallowed women in a wide variety of naked scenes of erotic debauchery. You sent hit-movies like *Straw Dogs*, in which the ultra-respectable intangibility of white womanhood, the sacredness of her marital status, was literally thrown to the dogs when Susan George was ravaged in a detailed slow-motion group-rape, illustrating the perverse pleasure that was to be derived, both by the victim and the assailant, from the degradation of forceful violation. In consequence, in the spirit of a copy-cat disposition, it became the fashion in African society for armed robbers to raid homes and, as a mark of the conqueror, ravage the madam of the house in the forced presence of her husband and children.

The Africans have come to understand that the great utopian atmosphere of ready-made London is charged with a constant mood of sex. There was the craze for 'hot pants', in which women started to flaunt their availability. There were fashions for low-cut blouses, skimpy skirts, the generally provocative mode of dressing calculated to arouse erotic passions. Several visiting liberated African females attempted to introduce these modes of dress in the earlier stages of the fashion, and took to their heels as they were chased and stoned all the way home by jeering crowds of youths. There was now a tacit decree passed that no friendship between the two sexes could properly be sealed without the nitty-gritty of bedroom frolics – either by hook or by crook.

The hoisting of the flag of free love, as described, was contemporaneous with the 'currency' splash of Nigeria's unique quality Sweet Bonny Light oil that took the society into the trillion-dollar league, with the promise that if properly managed with sound, disciplined leadership, she could attain a measure of power and status.

The thirst for Western values was subsequently amplified. But in the absence of two hundred years of industrial experience, taking short-cuts became the name of the game for survival. Hence Lord Queensberry was rudely shoved aside in his insistence on playing by the rules, paving the way for the triumph of the irrational and the unprincipled – rooted in a policy of quantity rather than quality for now. With the crucifix in one hand and a corresponding lip-service in church in their best Sunday wears, these patrons of quantity would clutch Satan's totem or fetish object in the other hand, such 'liberal' disposition rooted in the observation that Satan does not have a single salaried helper while the opposition employs a million. So they will dance in whichever direction the wind of fortune blows;

and in the case of Satan, the blood of men from human sacrifice will enhance the speedy inflow of funds from that oil.

I observe the innumerable flashy cars that pile along the pot-holed streets, acquired through the fly-by-night activities of their barely literate owners. As if in answer we see the decaying corpses of ritual slaughter abandoned on the dusty, unpaved waysides, their eyes, tongues and private parts having been removed for offerings at the devil's shrines to expedite material prosperity. Understandably, having graduated from bush to concrete, it may not be quite so romantic thereafter, for the euphoria of the oil boom in their native land has ushered in a culture of stampede and haphazard activities that would trample Lord Queensberry underfoot if he dared again to show his face with his notion of civilized rules for fair fighting. Who cares about a 200-year industrial experience to usher in the utopia of London, even if Her Majesty's Government ranks as our nation's greatest trading partner?

Hence in the hustle and bustle, toil and trouble, traffic on the chaotic streets and highways has become a game of dodgems, and the scale of injuries and fatalities surely attains global record heights. All imaginable consumer goods are being hawked on the pavements and sidewalks in feverish competition, rarely of the 'healthy' type, and passengers in a snail's pace go-slow are barracked in their vehicles. All hell is let loose as the 'beasts of the field' flee the bush-fire of poverty and 'Third World' status in general with less dignity than the crude oil that has bewitched their senses, miraculously defying the heat – which is like heat nowhere else in the world. It has begun its destruction of nerves, sanity, love-life, ability to reason, eating through flesh, bone and marrow, sapping the last vestiges of strength, energy and will, leaving a zombie-like impotence and listlessness in all but the exceptional.

And it is here that the strength of the African is exceptional; for when it is a question of money, everybody is of the same religion. In the obstreperous chaos, *everybody* knows - courtesy the miracle of Nigeria's newfound wealth, that money can do anything, and, in turn, everybody would be willing to do *anything* for money.

Only the Englishman has a monopoly of the universal snobbery that makes people think that they can be happy without money.

And what consumer goods do you have to offer, old hawker? Aha! Magazines that depict naked, bosomy white women on the front cover. That commodity is moving as briskly as the sachets of water that keep pedestrians from passing out from the heat.

CHAPTER 7

Dreams deferred

Yours Truly, engorged by the supposed entertainment value of the various branches of the love-game that he has explored in England, is often encouraged to reflect on the African scenario for a more objective study of a way of life established at a remote period in time, yet surviving side-by-side with a comparative utopia that should not – if supremacists are to be believed – be sharing the same planet. In my view the freedom to explore every avenue of pleasure that flesh in civilized English life has to offer, in an atmosphere of euphoria and peace, could not be possible without the ready-made security of effective law-enforcement that British society enjoys.

The impression that the Lord Jesus Christ had declared the appointment of these English islanders as his chosen people, as it once appeared during those good old days when the Englishman deferred to Christian dogma, is somewhat underlined by the deafening silence that greets one on arrival at London Heathrow Airport. There is a hallowed glory about this quietness that forbids even a pin to drop. It would require just the taking off of the shoes for the tacit deference to be complete, although the muffled footfalls along the carpeted corridors towards Immigration somehow serve to amplify the sacredness of the condition in which one finds oneself. A uniformed police officer is stationed at every turn, from the point of disembarkation through to Immigration, then to Customs, and all the way out to the Underground station. The message is clear even to the most unimaginative: that the secret of sustaining the beauty of this organized utopia is a strict regard for the rule of law, and no one is above it. For that reason one second of trouble will not visit any mortal of whatever hue for as many years as he opts to reside on the island if he is not one of troublesome disposition, and if he respects the Englishman's sense of privacy and strict minding of his business. To uphold this system, the Englishman places the police officer on a pedestal.

The conjectured observer who was earlier introduced to encounter the 'demerits' of a Third-World society now swings his lens away from Heathrow Airport to a much rowdier airport at night, south of the Sahara. He observes a visiting native's prudent decision to head for the nearest police headquarters to lodge a hefty sum in hard currency for safe keeping overnight. The young man is driven in a licensed airport taxi-saloon and the driver will wait to take him to the nearby military barracks, where he will spend the night with a cousin.

As the long minutes tick away, the driver is suddenly startled by two loud gunshots, and panics. Our observer knows what has happened. The police officers at the counter, devoured by greed over the size of the booty being entrusted to their safe keeping, confer in secret for several minutes before summoning the visitor to an inner room, where, without further ado, they dispatch him to the hereafter.

The taxi-driver speeds off to the military barracks, where he makes his report, and is able to locate the dead visitor's cousin. Subsequent enquiries conducted by top military personnel confirm the visitor's murder by police officers. The country is being ruled by a military junta, and instant military action is taken. The order from above is "shoot to kill", and fifteen police officers who have divided the spoils – including a Chief Superintendent – are shot dead without trial at point blank range. End of story.

Our observer scans the length and breadth of this savage dog-eat-dog society and sees a familiar pattern to the horror that he has witnessed. During a scene of political unrest, over thirty police officers are shot dead by militants, and their bodies burnt beyond recognition. Again and again scores of police officers are gunned down in armed robbery incidents, and the toll in police deaths in a year from crime exceeds six hundred. If just *one* policeman is killed by criminals in Europe, the shock-waves from the public's outrage would never subside.

Our observer recognises that south of the Sahara the public's disdain for the police derives from the general image of the force as a bunch of nationalised hoodlums, indistinguishable from the criminals whom they have been recruited to fight, and often a greater source of terror than crime by way of intimidation and extortion at every opportunity. Too often they are the cold-blooded murderers of resisting victims of their extortion, at times the secret sponsors of armed robbery operations as a get-rich-quick strategy that spills oceans of blood in its wake.

Disdain of the police is further registered by incidents of the stripping and caning of meddlesome police officers in motor parks by irate drivers and touts. A more grisly reprisal involved the slaughter and painstaking dismemberment of a middle-aged cop who had amassed a terrible record of frame-ups and extortion, and the subsequent abandonment of the heaped slices of his body outside a pepper-soup beer parlour joint.

The apparent failure of law enforcement, however, does serve to reflect the national character of a people still trying to slug their way out from the painful throes of transition, trapped in an imbroglio comparable to a whirlwind, hence in a hopeless situation where discipline becomes irksome. A corresponding thread of sameness permeates every facet of society, in every line of discipline, both in government and private circles.

Our observer, reflecting on this unedifying scenario, observes that in the get-rich-quick mania triggered like a tornado by oil wealth, a small coin before the eye hides all else from sight. The attendant lawlessness comes into sharper focus as having been perfected into a fine art, becoming second nature for a people who could not give a cuss about not having had two hundred years of industrial experience but are bent on making up for lost time by cutting corners. Demonstrating a flair for scam and criminality that is as much cultural as a tribute to individual initiative, they have applied this fine art to the export market, triggering a global outcry. Yet this nightmare ended up forming the *nouveau riche* in their society, recording legendary profits and, in the process, very nearly rendering a leading British bank insolvent. They may lack the English finesse and refinement to sanctify the glory of wealth, and their overall efforts at development may be copy-cat by comparison, such that every mistake in Europe becomes a new invention south of the Sahara; but, with their newfound wealth, they erect structures as fine as those in Europe, and bridge the generation gap by exposing their offspring to the privilege of quality European education. They themselves may lack basic educational qualification outside primary school, not having been privileged with the opportunity to travel offshore to secure academic accomplishment, but if, perchance, they triumph in elections for political office and would be required to furnish evidence of basic educational qualification to be eligible to serve the nation, they would buy at exorbitant prices bogus educational degrees from unscrupulous commercial universities in the US specially set up to address their requirements. And they can well afford it.

At the end of the day one finds a sizeable number of them as well-placed individuals, garbed in the finest clothing, chauffeured in flashy modern limousines, attempting to speak in a stiff mixture of pidgin and elementary nursery English and expressing themselves in barely literate sentences in written correspondence. Nobody will question them, because money speaks and they have it in abundance.

Hence the supposed imbecility of their Third-World status is counter-balanced by a maverick of unparalleled acuteness in the art of survival, clever rather than intelligent. But as a people, technologically speaking, they have been unable to manufacture even a pin.

Our conjectured observer cannot see, in this overall picture, how modern English practices could ever find acceptance, let alone appreciation and enjoyment, outside base commercial exploitation of the type that would shame the white Madonna rather than place her on a pedestal. Our observer is wont to say to me, "I'll continue to pray for you, because prayers will be what you need when you leave these shores. Meanwhile, give me a break while I enjoy the romantic side of bestiality."

At this point of his narrative, Yours Truly observes that in the wake of the oil-boom that has blessed his motherland, the romantic side of bestiality which is practised in England undergoes a radical change in his native environment, thanks to the uncountable golden opportunities that oil has ushered in. Just as the fashion in developed societies showed a semblance of catching on in Africa, it became a purely commercial affair among women who had been culturally prudish by comparison. The fire of 'bedroom' athleticism demonstrated by the Englishwoman, as stoked by the wintry chill of England, compared unfavourably with the laid-back tolerance of the African recipient in the lethargy-inducing heat south of the Sahara; and when finally she reaches the mountain-top, as it were, it is essentially the sole reward for a tiresome business that temporarily marginalises its procreative essence. Still, notwithstanding the decorum of diplomatic pretence, sex is like business – get to the point and get it over and done with. They are not in the mood, as defined by their culture, to have time for the European cliché of the love-stricken suitor and his partner, "I love, you, I love you, I love you!' No African would think of parting with such mechanical words, any more than the object of his affection would expect to hear them.

This attitude appeared to shape the general outlook of unlettered womanhood, and the gleam of solid cash (or goods in kind) remains the greatest inducement to adultery among even some ordinarily strict married women. There is little value in mere physical attraction for its own sake, and woe betide the misguided suitor who might perchance entertain the notion that the woman's acquiescence could come for nothing – in contrast with a sultry English wife who, notwithstanding the silk-lined financial security of her marital set-up, could readily have it off with the family chauffeur, say, if there is physical chemistry between them.

Hence erotic motivation on the part of the Englishwoman runs neck-and-neck, like parallel lines, with the same eagle-eyed passion for material inducement on the part of the female African as a basis for surrendering to male gratification. Each would feel contempt for the other's choice of 'bait' to be hooked, each charging the other with moral decadence.

Taking due cognisance of all this, I was not entertaining any ideas of settling down with my own 'soul sister' any time soon. But certain developments in this black/white boiling cauldron between the two groups caused me to reconsider. The war on AIDS had commenced in earnest. Dutifully the British Government, as a matter of policy, mounted a training programme to educate every Briton on the pandemic. In this regard the only racial group boldly proclaimed in leaflets as AIDS suspects, and so must not give blood, are "men and women who have had sex at any time since 1977 with men and women living in African countries, except those on the Mediterranean".

I saw red over this subtle wholesale blacklisting of every African for a disease that was initially blazed worldwide as having originated from America. The disease was first identified in 1981 in California and New York, where it perplexed doctors. In October 1986 it claimed the life of actor Rock Hudson at the age of only 59, heightening American awareness of its existence. From America the controversy and shame of the disease traversed the Atlantic and settled in Africa, whose people were then stigmatized as the arch-villains behind the spread of the disease.

I was afflicted with depression over this perceived injustice to my people. I now understood that my very blackness automatically presented *taboo* – whether or not I was a carrier of the dreaded disease. I felt personal affronted.

However, one blessing of my employment as a freelance journalist was the advantage of being able to keep my ear to the ground in order to acquire privileged information. One is constantly exchanging notes with colleagues and contacts in the press, over drinks at the pubs and in newspaper offices to submit stories. If I smouldered for a long time over the stigmatization of my African folk with the AIDs plague, as I did, other information gathered privately served to add fuel to fire. The London-based African male who has experienced the ecstasy in the bedroom with a white lady might be further impressed and titillated by the tendency of some women to go public with salacious details of their bedroom frolics - provided he was not depicted or identified in any way in any such exposure.

In the fashionable *pot-pourri* of offerings from the Englishman's castle, one could be bemused by the brow-raising exploits of sultry Gloria Barrett in her raunchy memoir *All My Lovers*. Another famous actress confessed to mankind through the high-paying *News of the World*, "I sinned to become a star", describing and naming a film director who 'signed her on' from a 'rear connection'. In the words of Mariella Novotny, "I can't wait for the next scandal to rock the political boat. One man's fuck is another man's tit-bit."

One might ask – whatever happened to the privacy laws and the sacredness of sharing a secret between just the two of you? But, and it's a big but, it appeared to be an unspoken European monopoly to go public with bedroom adventures, provided they were with European partners. A Senegalese jazz musician who was privileged to bed a celebrated and widely-revered princess from a towering European royal family (who shall, charitably, remain nameless) was chilled by a terse warning from undercover security operatives of painful summary execution if he went public with his royal adventure. That little homily on the wisdom of silence was well heeded, and later duly acknowledged with a generous sum by way of "Thanks for your cooperation."

Then a vivacious, ubiquitous and celebrated London-based Nigerian lady called Minah Uko (popularly nicknamed by the British press 'Minah Bird'), a dear friend of mine and from the same Nigerian ethnic group, was not so wise, and hence not so lucky. After uncountable bedroom frolics reaching heights of unspeakable perversion with others from high society, including the aristocracy, the scandalous details were recorded in book form, together with the original names of her secret lovers. Unhappily she was exposed to the truism that what is good for the white goose is not always good for the black gander. She learnt that lesson too late. Her decomposing remains were later found in her flat in the wake of her supposed disappearance abroad on holiday, and all copies of the book were withdrawn before the scandals revealed therein could see the light of day.

I was thrown into deep depression when I became privy to that poor woman's elimination, and brooded for a week to the point of shedding tears. Minah Bird's death precipitated the final decision to take my leave from these shores. One evening I slumped against the wall, head in hands, and roared like a lion, "Oh God, what am I still doing here? It's time to get out of this bloody country and go home!"

It had finally dawned on me that the pleasures of permissiveness in the paradise of England had their limits. Death could be the outcome for anyone, especially the person of midnight hue who had taken English refinement for granted. When push came to shove, there would always remain one rule for the white native and another for the black visitor. During the post-slavery milieu of supremacist attitudes in the US, the saying was "If you're brown, stick around. If you're black, get back." The image of contamination that blackness exuded in human form would never die down in the generality of the Aryan/Caucasian mind-set, and illicit love across the colour line was best conducted under the thickest cloak of secrecy. Anything to the contrary was essentially the preserve of high society white females.

My dismayed English better half tried to cheer me up. "But London has been good to you," she said. That was not the point. Even Muhammad Ali, after demolishing the fearsome George Foreman in Kinshasa, breezed through London on his way back to the US and lectured a group of visitors (myself among them) in my hotel suite on his favourite topic of race relations. "You black guys living here gotta start heading for home, man. You're in white man's country. This is his country. You ain't got no justification to complain if he don't want you here. Ain't no place for you here. You gotta go and develop your own, man."

When I had made that salient point in my second book, I was reviled roundly. But who could challenge 'The Greatest'?

Sure, London had been good to me. My better half and I had lived and breathed the luxury of middle-upper class existence, transported in three big, flashy Jaguar 420G saloons one after the other, enjoying glorious cross-country drives, wining and dining in fabulous eateries and at endless parties, jogging together across parks, enjoying the glory of ego-boosting limelight in newspaper gossip-columns, secure in steady income from several lines of discipline in the literary arts, connection with dear high-quality friends to spice the joys of good living, and comfortable in the civilising influence of Great Britain – to the extent that one could even fantasise about hitting the big time in the ready-made paradise of the Englishman. In that life of relative luxury and glamour, there was also the comfort of a fine home and the unforgettable eating experience from my wife's flair in the culinary arts. Oh, perchance to dream! The next port-of-call promised to be Heaven itself.

But the routine also had its limits, and no one was immune to rot setting in. In my case, my lingering thoughts of my African home environment continued to gnaw at my conscience for positive movement in that direction. There was a sense of duty to impart to my underprivileged countrymen the benefits of scholastic refinement gathered from the highest seat of learning. I well appreciated my wife's misgivings, which she would tearfully lament one day, "I knew that when you decided to go home it would be quits for our marriage," she said.

Even our conjectured observer appeared to be concerned, telepathically telling me in reference to the comparative 'jungle' of Third-World existence, "Only fools rush in where angels fear to tread." I replied defensively, "Half of our mistakes in life arise from feeling where we ought to think, and thinking where we ought to feel. I have something to offer my people, something from which I know they will benefit and which they will appreciate. Why should I stay here and be abstract?"

CHAPTER 8

Love across the colour line

As earlier confessed, unlike many of my compatriots of midnight hue, I cannot pretend that I was not afflicted by an obsession with the physical attractions of the Englishwoman during those memorable London days. It grew into a cancerous desire to possess one of my own, a longing which gnawed away at my sanity until I was forced to join that growing army of 'Afro-Saxons' who took one to wife, ultimately to return with her in tow to their African environment – pursuant to the illusion that the magic of such 'true love' with a European woman could never end.

Our conjectured observer was wont to remind me of a prevailing sore point in this matter. In the course of a visit home some years back, a group of a dozen female elder relations had requested an urgent meeting, during which they sought to remind me of the existence of an unspoken law not to betray our people by giving one's hand in matrimony to a white woman. This was not a people who naturally lived and breathed the English culture of minding your own business. Having extracted from me a smiling assurance that such would not happen, it became a matter of simply presenting practical evidence that promises were made to be broken. All they could do, in the face of such visual evidence, was to look on in speechless disbelief.

But what was this 'unspoken law' anyway? Essentially that my grandfather was royalty. He "enjoyed almost legendary wealth and power" and "wielded a power which a missionary compared with an Arab despot, and which it was extremely dangerous to disregard", a Professor of History recorded in a book. The said missionary also commented, "This particular chief would deserve a history to himself; for he was probably the only Igbo ruler whose word was law." (Igbo being one of Nigeria's three main ethnic groups). Another witness reported that through slavery and extortion, my much-feared grandfather "accumulated much wealth and became the greatest man who lived in those days... He married over forty wives".

The 'Almighty' Paramount Chief Onyeama, the Okuru Oha, the 1st of Agbaja (the largest Igbo sub-clan), travelled to England in 1924 for the British Empire Exhibition. Thereby he became the first Igbo man to go to England (his predecessors having gone offshore as slaves). With that visit to England and seeing the pedestal on which the white woman was placed and the 'excessive' freedom and sacredness attached to her womanhood, the Chief vented his displeasure in his will. It stipulated: "I direct that in the event of either of my sons marrying a European, he that so marries shall not inherit any benefits whatsoever under my will."

That expressed opposition to marriage across the colour line was the basic consideration upon which my extended family relations sought to sermonise against any breach of the taboo. My father came close to infringement with his betrothal to an English lady during his student days in London, but was spared by the technicality that he had not actually tied the nuptial knot, even though a son emerged from the cohabitation. That experience served to lay bare, as nothing else could, the 'jinx' or 'contagious effects' of European romantic love on the long-term African resident who should happen inadvertently and unwittingly to fall under its spell. It was an intrinsic part of European culture, and extremely difficult to resist.

One other cousin had been similarly 'jinxed' with that love spell and found himself inseparable from his heart-throb. He proceeded to take her back to his natural environment, and suffered the humiliation of being publicly assaulted by enraged masqueraders, who whipped the living daylights out of him before the horrified eyes of his fiancée. His mortal sin was the flouting of local custom, which forbade the presence of females in public during the two-day period of their 'roaming the streets', as it were. Women were supposed to be confined indoors, or, should they venture outside, flee swiftly back home on sighting any masquerader.

The cousin's fiancée was so traumatised by this experience that it precipitated, along with other prohibitive cultural considerations, the breakup of their relationship. It was right and fitting that her fiancé took the punishment, because he was wholly answerable. He was well cognisant of the rules, and should have kept his wife out of sight, knowing this was the period for the 'roaming' of the masqueraders. A local female offender would have been similarly whipped, her gender notwithstanding. But in this case the white hue of the offender was her saving grace. The white man was still psychologically feared in black Africa, and cases of physical assault of a white man by an African were rare.

As regards the controversial stipulation in my grandfather's will, I held fast to a dissenting opinion. The will did not expressly or by implication extend to generations unborn. It was specifically referable to the Chief's sons. But the apparent disregard for this consideration, reflected in the group approach to myself, was eloquent proclamation of the invisible 'small print' of a blanket ban.

Be that as it may, all along it had seemed to me that the logical end of infatuation with the physical attributes of the white woman would have to be marriage. During my days of youthful exuberance, there was the added thrill of speculating about actually siring a child from a white female. Yet the initial steps I took in that direction did not yield the imagined dividends of everlasting fulfilment. Following up on the very first conquest, at the age of eighteen, of a female English partner a year older than me, the thrill of 'following up' with a love-letter was answered with the discouraging rebuke, "I think that night we both showed ourselves to be very, very immature indeed, and I hope it will be enough for me to say that I never want to see you or hear from you again."

Devastated, I persevered with every attempt at reassurance. Her response was more explanatory, but no less unrelenting: "That first time I went with you, I felt a tart; and each time I hear from you, I still feel like a tart. You were so self-absorbed and self-satisfied that you never even noticed my feelings about what happened. You obviously did not consider how it would be to give birth to a child who would never be properly loved. It was one big mistake from beginning to end, and now it really has finished."

Humiliated by the idea of being cuckolded by his first white woman, I pined away in misery. Ultimately I plucked up some courage and adopted the philosophy of my favourite sage, Israel Zangwill: "Nothing can be more digestive after a good dinner than a spirited denunciation of the sinfulness of eating it."

I was comforted by another successful 'fishing' expedition at Speakers' Corner, Hyde Park, where so many competitors of my kind with the same one-track-mind landed impressive catches whose gleam of white skin near blinded one. Maybe it was my colour and size (6ft. 2½ins and a brawny 15 stone), with the possible addition of polished English diction, which landed the prized catches. Later I would decide it was just Mother Luck, because many of my competitors, though bigger than me and of a deeper shade of black, expressed themselves in barely literate sentences, yet recorded quality catches that aroused my envy.

Mother Luck presented real Danish butter as the next course, of a quality and succulence that surpassed Lurpak. Our intimacy endured for several meaningful months in physical terms, and for over 50 years along memory lane in correspondence and on the social network. Yet it was interrupted, and at first seemingly terminated, early on by my flamenco dancing with a partner from Spain's coastal town San Sebastian, who riveted attention at every turn, looking as if she could be the daughter of screen goddess Sophia Loren. She had identical features – the same raven-black flowing hair of silk texture, framing a prominent uplifted face, dark eyes, pouting lips, a cheeky cleft of the chin, and the same secret (but inadvertent) seductiveness reflecting in the depths of smiling eyes. But Sophia Loren was Italian and famously well-endowed figure-wise; this young girl was fragile and petite, trim as a blackbird, and eminently Spanish. It was a classic merging of Beauty and the Beast, giving rise to the occasional thrilling fantasy of a great rutting black monster victimising a poor helpless white victim. I was hopelessly in love, a feeling that was reciprocated with passion. After several glorious months in shared rented accommodation, engagement rings were purchased and fixed on fingers, and a pregnancy was announced. I luxuriated in the thrilling prospect of a real-life black-white child. My expectant fiancée rushed off to San Sebastian to announce the good news to her family. She was, after all, a legal adult at 21, a little over a year older than I was.

The news landed on her family about as gently as a Hiroshima bomb. Her father aged a century overnight and suffered a near-heart attack. Her mother shrieked blue murder. Her brother, mildly startled, was also tickled, and he teased her and told his friends about his 'errant' sister's role in a real-life drama performance of a black Romeo and a white Juliet. The outrage for the family was rooted in the unthinkable prospect of a black fiancé.

The end result was that amid her tearful protests, her incensed mother hauled her off by the scruff of the neck to London and an abortion clinic. As a staunchly Roman Catholic family, the shame of an abortion on their home soil did not bear thinking about. Thereafter Mama hired a vehicle in a feverish search to confront her daughter's black lover and speak her mind to him, no doubt with the most eloquent Spanish obscenities. My faithful 'partner in crime' tipped me off by phone about the ensuing search, and I demonstrated my adroitness in the hide-and-seek game. Every sighting from the back seat of the car of a brawny-looking black man would elicit an angry challenge from Mama, "Is that him?"

Ultimately my devastated fiancée stole out into the night for a meeting at a secret location and, in the shadows of a shopping area, tearfully reported, "The baby has gone, Charlie."

I died from this double loss. Somehow, after a long period of time, I resurrected myself, but I was never quite the same man. I never saw her again.

Our conjectured observer, observing Yours Truly in the light of the foregoing, is deeply compassionate. Our observer has taken a long, hard look at the author's 22-year sojourn in the refining paradise of England and the fine breeding that accrued therefrom. It culminated in my marriage to the finest of English womanhood, both in class and feminine allure. Her femininity was bewitching in every consideration, with piercing dark eyes, delicate features, sensuous quivering lips and a spellbinding figure. There was a hint of mystery in the partnership which I devoted several years to trying in vain to decipher. The marriage took place in 1977, on the 11th day of the 11th month, to an English lady 11 years older than I was. Mind you, by this time I had learned to appreciate the virtues of 'mature wine' against younger, fresher, offerings, as it were.

This monumental advantage in the age difference between us was reflected in the maturity gained by my outlook in the challenges of life. In that regard my better half presented something of a mother figure, which yielded uncountable benefits by way of the benefits of home living, good housekeeping and attitudes in interaction with the rest of the human race. However a monumental disadvantage in the union was the existence of a gynaecological anomaly that denied me the offspring I would have treasured from her 'white womanhood' almost as much as her magnetic humane personality. I was too jinxed by her beauty and attendant human attributes to attach too much relevance to that very important consideration.

Her general strictness as regards decorum in every feature of human life – good manners and social etiquette, good hygiene, diplomacy, civilised eating at the dining-table – and her eye for perfection in maintaining a spick-and-span atmosphere in the home left no room for mistakes. I saw these qualities as a gift from the gods. We had a tacit understanding that she ruled supreme as regards matters domestic, while I was accorded the privilege of overall control as the man of the house. When contention reared its head over any matter, and degenerated to raised voices and ended with her tears, invariably it was settled by the joys of my superior physical strength, intoxicated by the thrill of dominance, and final settlement by passionate bedroom frolics, be it on the dining-table, in the living-room armchair, or on the wide double bed.

The reality of not being able to have a biological child with her made me resolve to enjoy what was available while it lasted. As if divining that resolve, I enjoyed unfettered access to ravenous feastings of erotic variety whenever I wanted them. If excessive libido was compensated with a reciprocal scale of give-and-take in 'nympho' language, could one possibly afford the constant changing of bed-springs – with the cost of living as it was? In the final analysis, who could possibly imagine that London had not been good to me in a union that was too good to be true?

The overriding glory of that marital union was the beauty of loving a real-life human being as opposed to a white woman, or a sex object - and vice-versa. It was like an awakening to a new reality that other attributes of a person existed outside of physical attraction and colour. Our love was almost religious, and after a period in time, all the different components of attraction, divined by the human touch, merged into a magic of indivisible oneness. We were inseparable, doing virtually everything together, going everywhere together. The marriage provided a level of happiness and fulfilment that seemed too good to be true.

Our observer considered my happy-go-lucky resignation to the atheistic drift that tends to follow over-indulgence in the pleasures of European womanhood, shakes his head and nods in awful acknowledgement, "Oh boy, you are in deep trouble." For the atheistic drift had progressed to a level where the existence of God had long left my consciousness, and only wedding celebrations and funerals of friends brought to memory the vague notion that such a thing as a deity exists.

So, against the pleadings even of my English better half, we joined the long column of other mixed couples bound 'homeward' to develop Africa. All sex in England and no hard work in Africa would not make for global peace, but then, in Africa, when the indigene talks of his love for his country, he leaves you in no doubt that he expects to be paid for it. Hence, for our molly-coddled Yours Truly and his better half, there is no way of receiving payment for patriotic services rendered. The tidal wave of illiteracy overwhelms the ripples of English-trained African manpower; the immense power of the irrational swamps the semblance of rationality.

One is now compelled to drop one's English guard with the decisive resolve that when he encounters a lion he should roar, but when he meets an ass he should just bray. As there are more lions than asses, one is soon forced to appreciate that the problem with shouting at a six-year old is that in no time at all, you begin to sound like a six-year old. The English better half cannot – and will not – conceive that true love could ever involve adopting a culture a thousand years away in time, many generations apart, in which romantic love is at best a variety of farce (for now, at least).

Our dismayed observer calls me to the window: "Come and take a look at this!" Lo and behold, the Good Lord has created a path between the waves of the Atlantic, solidifying them into a wall-like firmness (as He did for Moses and the children of Israel) for the frustrated population of mixed couples to escape back to the sanctuary of England. "Look, there she goes," shouts our observer, pointing out Yours Truly's better half among them, escaping without him, having failed in her desperate bid to persuade him by pleading, "Please, let's go back to London and carry on. There is no decent life here."

"Oh dear," commiserates our observer as he shoots a glance at a heart-broken Yours Truly. "I can't believe it! Look at your educated people abandoning all they have just to go back to a culture of love in a nation that has only coal to offer as a natural resource. Look at all they're leaving behind – you have oil, you have gas, you have coal of the highest premium, you have bitumen, you have timber, you have aluminium ore, you have tin, you have diamonds, you have gold, you have limestone, you have salt, lead, copper, sand, silica, zinc coal, you have nuts, fruits cocoa... You have so much going for you. It's just a matter of careful planning, patriotic patience, sacrifice and hard work – that's all; and with all that western-trained manpower, the sky will be your limit in no time at all. You can't just ignore all these assets and confine your interests to oil. Rome was hardly built in a day. It's all very upsetting."

Yours Truly offers a defensive explanation. "This development appears to reflect God's perfect justice. There can be no one-sided profit whereby the beneficiaries of quality education and refinement offshore should, for that reason alone, become the sole reapers of the natural resources of a developing society. The unlettered indigenes have the entitlement to enjoy the national cake in the way best known to them; and where the population of the illiterate dwarfs the small school of the learned, they would have no choice but to stamp the rules of Lord Queensberry underfoot if they expect to enjoy their own slices of the cake. The learned, in turn, would have no option but to flee and be contented with serving in Paradise. They would see, and *have* seen, true hell if they attempt to slug it out with savages in the fiery furnace that is their fatherland. That's why you're seeing those endless flights across the Atlantic."

"And look at all those delicious ripe cashew fruits falling to the ground and being left to rot away in your country," exclaims our observer. "Couldn't they be harvested and sold? What a waste."

"They were right in putting romantic love into books," confesses

Yours Truly. "Outside London, it couldn't live anywhere else – certainly not in Africa."

"Mmm," our observer muses, inclined to agree.

"I'm afraid an Afro-Saxon goes crazy when he is in love with a European woman," says Yours Truly, sadly shaking his head. "The magic of that love is so rooted in the couple's ignorance that it can never end."

CHAPTER 9

For love of a better half

If the details of my marriage to an Englishwoman could be compared, albeit vaguely, with a feature of Robert Graves' wartime memoir *Goodbye to All That* "where I had recently broken a good many conventions", it would not be inappropriate to reflect on where, how and when I embarked on my 'irregular' marital adventure. The need for such information becomes more compelling in the light of a communication received some 40 years after the traumatic parting of ways. That Letter from an Ex-Wife, as it could be described, travelled down memory lane to that night and place where it all started: not in London, but in the ironic scenario of a real-life African location. The communication laid bare my former spouse's flair for the poetic arts in relation to the generality of innate beauty which the duo shared during their memorable times together...

> *The warmth of a balmy African night,*
> *The moon high and very bright.*
> *Rhythmic music filled the air,*
> *Then I saw you standing there tall and debonair*
> *Hands outstretched to hold me tight,*

We danced away that balmy night.
We whirled and twirled around the floor,
A man I had never met before.
We went from there to deeper depths,
A time remembered with loving regrets...
An unfinished symphony.

The place is Lagos, Nigeria's bustling capital, the year 1977. Elegant only on its south-east side, a façade of ultra-modern skyscrapers is deposited in the environs of a festering fly-blown slum. Here a vast number of Lagosians live in a sleazy shanty-town existence that fails to keep them dry when it rains. *Lagos...* figuratively speaking, it hits the nostrils before the eyes. During daylight hours it is a hurly-burly of activity, scourged by stifling traffic congestion. The Government had tackled the traffic problem by making it law that cars beginning with odd and even numbers must be used on alternate days. Trust the acuteness of the wealthy Nigerian citizen, who tackled that problem by purchasing two cars, one beginning with an odd number, the other with an even one. In consequence the traffic problem doubled.

During this period, Nigeria was on its best behaviour, with thousands of artists and tourists from all over Africa and its diaspora drawn to luxuriate in the country's ambitious festival of arts, music, dance, literature and culture to be held in Lagos. Its acronym, FESTAC, stood for 'Festival of Black Arts and Culture'.

As the old taxi groans and bumps uncomfortably along the pitted roads, one is conscious of that sinking feeling as one sees the clear signs of retrogression. Sure, there are a few signs of progress – flashy cars have virtually replaced bicycles, psychedelic Western wear of varying impressive assortments is evident on the young. But the dividends do not appear to extend further. Almost everything is done in the open – trading, sleeping, gossiping, cooking, eating, board-games, conducted on the wayside or in courtyards – within feet of the open gutters. There is an assortment of garbage piled up in mountainous bulk, there are great puddles of stagnant water with their putrefying stench, germ-carrying flies, and pollution from the exhaust fumes of the countless age-worn lorries and buses. Careless people and cars have fallen into these gutters during rain-floods. A group of women dressed in national costumes and jewellery that must have cost a fortune, outwardly conveying the impression of wealth and high-class respectability, return home to hovels whose facades are decorated by heaps of rubbish.

Sewage stench is the main smell of Lagos, haunting one like a curse at almost every turn. The only difference between seeing and inhaling it all again now and when I left the country for Britain in 1959 is that it has worsened beyond imagination. This is explicable, one supposes, in that the population of the city has more than quadrupled since then in the wake of constant movement from rural locations to the urban areas. A newspaper photograph records an immaculately dressed well-to-do citizen who could not drive his Mercedes saloon through the front gate because of the rubbish piled on the wayside.

Yet a middle-aged female tourist from Barbados exults, in breezy candour, "It feels just like being at home. I don't feel like a guest at all. The only difference between here and Barbados is that this is much bigger." One could understand (and forgive) this state of affairs in her country, the Caribbean Islands being comparatively poor, but Nigeria was among the wealthiest nations in the world, hoisted by supreme quality oil to the peak of global envy and demand.

After a couple of days, one becomes immune to the eyesores and nauseous smells. Matters are not helped by the blame game whereby one ethnic group blames the unsavoury cultural lifestyle of another for the national filth. No worthwhile solution is offered to enforce the hygiene laws which are in existence. Priority has been given to a national stampede along a new 'fast lane' to extract one's own pound of flesh from the windfall of oil.

One thinks wistfully of the example of Singapore as the world's cleanest city. Could not such harsh laws be introduced in "our dear own native land" (second line of our national anthem) to prohibit even the unintentional dropping of mere cigarette ash in the streets, with a punitive penalty of a hefty fine or a six-month prison sentence for offenders, no matter how highly placed? Enormous warning signs could be erected at all airports warning visitors of these stringent hygiene laws. It is something of an eye-opener to learn that not one speck of litter can be seen in the streets of Singapore as a result of its penalties. They are always enforced strictly, irrespective of the status of the offender, and that is why Singapore enjoys the reputation of the world's cleanest city. What stops "our own dear native land" from adopting that principle tomorrow?

Meanwhile Nigeria is possessed by FESTAC fever – because the uncountable numbers of foreign business tourists converging on Lagos are really there just to make *money!* Who wants to know about art in the face of gushing oil? Everybody just raises a brief eyebrow at the city's hygiene challenges, even if subtly they are holding their breath. The government's stunning extravagance of a £100m investment in the preparations and execution of the festivities, with more millions piled into another event the following year called 'The International Trade Fair', seemed almost like a cover-up, an attempt at reassurance that the domestic essentials would be taken care of and that the government had the capacity to do it. The print and electronic media featured almost nothing else except the festivities of FESTAC, and the government had the bright idea to amplify the well-worn cliché *BLACK IS BEAUTIFUL, I'M BLACK AND PROUD* as the perfect bait to draw the local and international crowds from both sides of the colour divide. A windfall from the celebration of arts was 'FESTAC Town', which would initially house the profusion of performers. Thereafter it provided accommodation for ordinary Lagosians in state-of-the-art abodes, moved from their previous hovels. Full marks to the government!

An ideal conducive atmosphere for visitors coming to FESTAC to unwind and relax was to be found in exclusive hotels on the island. In one of the more exotic settings, with an open bar enclosure amid palm-trees and live-band playing calypso music, Yours Truly met the lady who was to be his wife. That development might not have come to pass had I not summoned the courage and audacity to approach her table, where she was seated with an elderly Portuguese friend and a Nigerian male escort, and request a dance. She had struck me as the most beautiful woman he had ever seen. She obliged, and in the course of our dance, remarked upon my impeccable English diction. She asked where I had gone to school. I hedged awkwardly, and revealed that it was a school near Windsor in the county of Berkshire, England.

"It wasn't Eton by any chance, was it?" she pressed further.

"Something like that," I confessed cagily.

"Oh!" she declared. "You're not by any chance the one who wrote a book about it, are you?"

"I'm afraid so."

"You're a pretty famous guy," she said.

"Maybe for all the wrong reasons."

"Why is it that almost every former Eton pupil I've met hates to disclose the name of the school where they were groomed?"

"An unspoken deference to the monument of modesty, you could say. It's too sacred a name to bandy around."

She was enchanted. I was overawed by her beauty, the softness of her contralto voice, her schooled down-to-earth receptiveness.

She was in Lagos to celebrate FESTAC with an elderly Portuguese journalist, whom she was chaperoning. She worked for him part-time as a widely-travelled researcher, and had lost count of the number of marriage proposals she had received. Telephone numbers were exchanged. Introductions were made. I was returning to London before them.

When we linked up there some weeks later, I was made to appreciate, forcibly, that she was not your ordinary pick-up. It took a long time before the ice was finally broken, thawed by the heat of the passion that consumed us both. This happened too soon for her liking, and she would often remind me, "I wish you had known me some years back. You would have just given up, as every other suitor did." Even her amazed retired parents would remark, "I can't believe we'd ever live to see Aileen so mastered."

I felt honoured, but more uplifted by our reciprocal feelings of love. I found her well-versed in the fine art of taking and giving physical love, a shrewd, subtle aristocrat in the love game. I believed I was in heaven. Within a matter of months, I was making vague proposals of marriage. As the shrewd judge of character that she was, she laughed and said, "If I agreed to marry you, you would be terrified."

She was probably correct if a white wedding was involved, because a crowd of passing pedestrians would surely stop to stare at these newly-weds as we emerged from the church. While I appreciated the limelight to a certain degree and was happy to be present where the news was (especially viewed from the perspective of a journalist and a novelist), it would be a whole different ball game when such very personal intimacy as a white wedding was involved. I did not feel cut-out for taking centre stage in such a focus of public attention. So we two love-birds settled for a Registry Office marriage in West London.

The Daily Express of London made a meal of the marriage on its gossip page, *William Hickey*. Newspapers in Nigeria reproduced the story. My clan back home was not immediately prepared to listen to my glowing testimonials on the unimpeachable integrity of the woman I had married. A cousin who had returned from a visit home telephoned to say that many were distressed that I had broken my promise to the wives (as earlier referred to). The only real support came from my father, now retired as a judge at the International Court of Justice in The Hague, Holland. Taking pains to point out possible areas of discord as regards the matter of mixed marriages, the old man's conclusion was uplifting. "I really wish you and Aileen the very best in the years ahead, and I really mean this. Of course, my home is your home."

My attitude towards the mounting opposition was one largely of indifference. I had my life to lead, and certainly I was not prepared to conduct my life to suit the purposes of so-called relatives who had shown no real interest in my welfare over the years.

Come Christmas that year, I took my better half to Nigeria for a month's holiday. Almost all my relatives took to her, thanks to their feelings of respect and awe towards the considerable influence wielded by my father the Judge. This included, would you believe, the female members of the group who had tried to dissuade me from marrying across the colour line. I did not need to stretch my imagination to imagine the snide remarks that would be made behind our back. So I had to maintain the traditional stiff-upper-lip as I watched my better half pawed, hugged and kissed, held and felt in the name of greeting and hospitality. I had to endure the subtle passes, gushing charm, crude forwardness, and the sarcastically gleeful proclamation, "This is *our* wife!" This utterance is a passing reference to the attitude that any wife married by the traditional custom of wine-carrying and dowry payment becomes a wife to all members of her husband's extended family. For me this burlesque of diplomacy was precisely that – a show. This fact would be divined by their utterances when the marriage was later dissolved.

My attempt to demonstrate the tolerant smile of English decorum against such theatrics was betrayed by the blatant provocation of a converted demon in a supermarket. He accused my better half of brushing against him, ranting "I have had a white woman in London just like you!" It took a vast amount of patience not to strangle him. He escaped with a well-presented delivery of invectives and was threatened with death as he was pushed away.

To the surprise of many, my wife was not the white woman they had thought would confine herself to the safety of Daddy's luxurious villa, afraid or too 'superior' to venture out by herself and mix with the so-called yokels. She was not the white woman who could be seen only under the protective wing of her husband. Indeed, after barely two days in the 'bush' that was my home, she was no longer a white woman, but a woman! She was now "one of us". Nor was she just my wife: when folks asked her whereabouts, the question was now, "Where is our wife?" The ease and avidity with which she tried to adapt to the people's ways, some of which most Westerners would have found intolerable, was remarkable, and it raised some amazed eyebrows.

My home was a traditional community beautified by dappled,

shadowy forests, sandy soil and palm trees. Numerous scattered farmsteads, with haphazard plantings of beans, maize, yam and cassava, fed the larger population of farmers and traders. Most lived on a subsistence level in thatch-bungalows, surrounded by tree-shaded courtyards in which bleating goats, scratching poultry and playful sparsely-clad children supplied almost all everyday activities outside the farms. Every now and again lunatic drivers sped along the treacherous uneven dirt tracks. A few Western-style buildings of breath-taking beauty which belong to well-to-do 'been-tos' sat solid and pretentious, overlooking their rustic counterparts of a thousand years away in time.

My wife could not believe that a luxurious villa like Daddy's could be deposited in such 'primitive' surroundings, with its onyx tables, crystal chandeliers and Indian carpets. She observed that it was like something out of a fairy-tale: suddenly, far off the beaten track, one was confronted with high walls and wrought-iron gates, concealing the gravel path and beautiful well-preserved perfumed gardens within. When it was dark a powerful plant supplied adequate lighting, in contrast with the rest of the community, which had not yet been blessed with electricity. The darkness was ominously black in the absence of the moon, and charged with the strident shrieks of nocturnal creatures. Only flickering candles and kerosene lamps permitted visibility to the thatch-roofed bungalows.

Outside on the dirt track the pedestrian must make his way with the power of sheer memory; and if one chanced upon him with the aid of a torch, one would be convinced he could see in the dark. One night my wife and I forgot our torch when they visited an uncle; it was with great apprehension that we felt our way gingerly home, terrified of stepping on a snake or a pot-hole, taking treble the time to arrive home. On our way, we almost froze with shock when a figure suddenly loomed past. It was a young native, who disappeared with the silence and speed with which he had appeared, with no word to them, but with a sure-footedness that was incredible.

The stark contrast in living standards between the 'haves' and 'have-nots' in Africa's traditional communities struck a sad note for my better half, who always identified with the plight of the underprivileged. She reached out to the semi-naked children who would sprint forward in their dozens to welcome her in public places, vying with each other to hold her hands. All had deprivation scrawled on their appearance: mucus dripped from nostrils, sores festered, attended by flies but not by their parents, the sandy soil having discoloured their bodies. Their malnourishment was underscored by physiques that had been retarded by any meaningful development in contrast to age, some bloated stomachs pointing to malnutrition. And to think they were all my relatives.

My wife's tears over the horrors of this 'Third-World' life completely drowned the holiday spirit. Those horrors empowered me to resolve to protect her at every turn, to the amusement of drivers and passengers of both private and commercial vehicles as we strode hand-in-hand along unpaved sidewalks. They would poke out their heads and shout "Hold her tighter, she's escaping from you!" in Igbo.

Admittedly it is a rare sight. A chauffeur-driven limousine was expected to ferry a white lady.

More horrors reflecting Third-World existence greeted us at Lagos Airport. The check-in lounge was jam-packed with a crowd of near-hysterical passengers, and the din as one approached hit us like a blast. First I found my wife somewhere away from the 'madding' crowd to sit, then tried to join the 'non-queue' to check in our luggage and get our boarding passes. Before long I was caught in the raucous shoving as tempers boiled and fisticuffs brewed. The airport officials were engaged in their notorious pastime of hoarding seats on the plane at the expense and frustration of travellers, who would be expected to fork out up to three times the normal price to secure a seat. These travellers fall into two categories: those who go to the airport in the hope of finding an available seat, and ticket-holders. The former are given preferential treatment because they are prepared not only to pay for a seat, but to part with enormous bribes to secure one. The practice is both encouraged and condoned by airport officials, and the outcome is a fraudulent game out of which the 'OK' ticket holders invariably emerge the losers. "OK ticket! OK ticket!" is the roar that cannons from over twenty mouths at the check-in desk, behind which the indifferent officials are mercifully separated from a potential lynch-mob by a strong wire-netting. Like wild animals people claw their way up this netting in their frustration, many trying to queue-barge, and others fighting and screaming to attract attention. A thunderous slap that must have been heard in heaven lands on somebody's face, somebody's irate finger pokes another's eye, abuse and oaths resound, fists fly, a suitcase lands on someone's head. Total pandemonium resounds, fired by the sweltering heat.

I tried to visualise the same mayhem in the unlikely setting of London Heathrow, UK, and imagined the white officials fleeing for dear life despite the protective wire-netting; I imagined the prompt arrival of truncheon-wielding police officers wading in to control the riotous situation. But this was Africa, and these were Africans. The officials were hardly mindful of the mass hysteria before them, and the few policemen who casually popped in and out were indifferent: they would get their own 'kick-backs'.

Next moment came the announcement everybody has been

dreading: "This flight is now closed." There was much wailing and gnashing of teeth. Some seventy passengers, ourselves included, had already bought tickets, but bribes had secured all the boarding passes. Vociferous ticket-holders complained of having spent three nights trying to catch flights, having lost their earlier flights to bribery. I was more concerned about the health of my better half, who was suffering from fluid retention in her ankles. She had to sit it out while I struggled into the restricted area to contribute to the storm of collective outrage, but at the end of the day I was forced to part with hard currency as a bribe, paid to a recommended go-between who disappeared and ultimately reappeared with the required boarding passes.

A similar challenge awaited us when changing our currency at the bank. An intimidating queue was moving at a snail's pace, in the absence of a cooling system, thanks to the 'traditional' power cuts that had become part of life. After a sweltering one-hour wait, a loud-mouthed bank official was overheard telling somebody, "You could end up spending three hours in this queue unless you play your cards right." Whereupon I loosened that traditional stiff-upper lip, charged at the loud-mouth, and there followed a hideous exchange of invective, riveting universal attention and summoning the anxious manager out of his office. I pointed to my seated better half. "We have not come all the way back from Europe to encounter this kind of criminal conspiracy you people practise here," I said.

The manager was full of apologies, and made a show of berating the errant official with the ominous instruction, "I will deal with you later." He invited us into his office. "That's what our society needs," he remarked to her as we took our leave, "decisive leadership."

In the light of these experiences, I did not feel ready to depart the shores of Britain for Africa any time soon. My wife seemed happy with that, even though she was always ready to make excuses for my people's painful efforts at development. I felt that I would require a whole new world of initiation before I could properly adapt and fit into the African scheme of things. I could only visualise a best-case scenario that would see me coming and going, like a yoyo, in between two homes, a habitual globe-trotter.

CHAPTER 10

The agony

Six full months elapsed before my wife, stricken with despondency since our departure from Britain, left for the UK with the intention of sorting out uncompleted domestic duties in our London home. To start with there was the pain of having to sleep in separate beds in our Lagos hotel, luxurious as it was. It seemed like a symbolic declaration, a preparatory beginning and a reminder of the inevitability of the wider division that would terminate our union on a permanent basis. A haunting sense of foreboding persisted, bringing with it a corroding and humiliating fear.

Not even the limelight that followed in the wake of the 'banquet' the Nigerian print and electronic media provided over the homecoming of the *Nigger at Eton*, with the additional spice of the publication of my new novel *Revenge of the Medicine Man* by the UK mass paperback publishers Sphere Books and now available in Nigeria to rave reviews, could dispel the gathering grey clouds of uncertainty over the future.

The initial plans to set up a book publishing company financed by an oil tycoon, having raised high hopes of quality life-style in the international setting of Lagos away from the prying intrusiveness of Yours Truly's Igbo people in the faraway east, dimmed when the prospective majority shareholder pulled out from the deal with claims of cash-flow restrictions. We were now left with the daunting challenge of having to start more or less from scratch, moving the company's initial office location inside the five-star Federal Palace Hotel in Victoria Island, Lagos, to my home town in Enugu, the traditional headquarters of the genus Igbo of the Lower Niger. It was a glorified one-horse town in which even car numbers were preserved in memory, and gossip, almost wholly malicious, reigned supreme as the most popular pastime.

We were both aware of the high premium that the African placed on the abundance of children in a marriage, to say nothing about the people's basic misgivings as regards the practice of mixed marriage in the first place. But the dilemma I faced on that score remained a closely guarded secret between me and my better half – and to Daddy, who was disquieted by the situation.

After setting up and equipping an office-cum-home in a lovely tree-lined haven of the rowdy metropolis, my wife jetted off to London with an agreed date when she would return. The arrangement was that I would travel to London on business and return with her. But I remained restless, harbouring a gnawing fear that she might not be planning to come back. Two days before I left, I phoned her and my fears were horribly realised.

"You are coming back with me, aren't you?" I asked.

There was palpable hesitation on the line. Then she declared, "No".

A cloud blotted out the sun, and my heart sank. From that moment, nothing in my life seemed to have any meaning any more.

I presented myself at my father's law chambers the following morning, grief-stricken, and broke the news to the old man. Daddy's features registered shock, but I would swear that I detected a covert smile on his lips. It passed quickly, and he appeared to commiserate. By way of comfort he said he would send his driver to chauffeur me to the airport in the morning and collect me there on my return from London. I was to learn that immediately after I left, the old man picked up his phone and rang the most senior and influential member of *Umuada* (the group of married aunts sired from the polygamous Onyeama family) to announce the good news: "Dillibe's wife has left for good."

"You don't mean it? Oh, God be praised!"

The news circulated like wildfire in the Enugu metropolis, and pretty well all members of my extended family chorused "Alleluja"!

An influential family friend who was to become an elected Governor reassured the despondent Yours Truly, "You've lost nothing. No Onyeama son should marry a white woman, most especially you. Any beautiful local girl that takes your fancy, go ahead and marry her by local custom. Cheer up."

A cousin, a top-ranking London-trained lawyer, presented a less decorous proposal in tactless jest: "Look for a local girl to marry, and in the meantime fuck as many girls as you can to get that woman out of your system."

Others were more caustic in their dismissal of the runaway English wife, contemptuous that their educated kith and kin could be lured away from the challenge of patriotic nation-building in the name of English love, and exasperated in their failed efforts to dispel the clouds of grief choking Yours Truly. "Is she the Virgin Mary or do her private parts conceal a bar of gold?"

"You don't know what God has done for you by liberating you from a white wife," declared another member of the extended family who was celebrating over the news of her departure. "The last thing we want is the desecration of our culture with offspring of sexual perversion."

I was appalled, to say the least, by the total absence of any sympathy over my loss and the venom that my beloved had attracted. I spared no words in rising stoutly to her defence at every criticism, in many cases delivering myself of unprintable abuse that earned me their eternal enmity.

I felt no regret for the pain inflicted by my barbed words. Spiritually I had not been unmindful of the subterranean opposition of my people to marriage across the colour line, in spite of their feigned smiles and words in my wife's presence – just as I was aware that a significant number of white people offshore harboured the same misgivings. But many couples went ahead and damned the consequences, and it had worked for them. Back here at home there were a number of mixed marriages, where the wives had formed themselves into a group solidarity called 'Nigerwives', which had survived the test of time.

It was the worst period of my life, and the best part of eternity had passed before I could fully come down to earth again. In an effort to preserve what little sanity I had left, I put a distance between myself and my people. As if possibly divining this resolve, my undivided commitment to hard work enabled me to take my country's publishing industry by storm with unique PR strategies that attracted good press, exalted my reputation and recorded handsome fees with brisk sales of compelling new titles. My endeavours , enriched by an industrious office staff and a creative sales team, ushered in opportunities for a ubiquitous existence through globe-trotting business travel – most enjoyable. I luxuriated in the glamour and business success that accrued from my company's participation in the Frankfurt Book Fair, Germany, in San Francisco for the American Book Convention, and in good old England for the London Book Fair.

In such instances, flashes of the old life of luxury and glamour left behind in London after my final return to Africa were relived over many glasses of champagne and succulent dishes consumed at innumerable cocktail parties, dinners and sight-seeing tours, all rounded off by the sealing of new business connections. It goes without saying that a generous offering of milk-white females succumbed to the right degree of patient and imaginative persuasion. The German women personified the formidable reputation of their people as avowed workaholics through bedroom wrestling. The Americans were the loudest and wildest, but the British retained that characteristic cultural finesse that placed them above the madding crowd, betraying suppressed guilt and self-control after surrender. But none of them seemed able to provide the magic experienced with my wife in that universal game of give-and-take, rekindled every time I passed through London.

At the end of the day, after an amicable divorce that saw us return to our former matrimonial home for a final good-bye in word and deed, I came fully down to earth. I became a son of the soil, and in due course was blessed with four boys and two girls. And that was that.

God, indeed, appeared to be the final arbiter who pulled asunder what was put together by man in that modern matrimonial chamber of a London Registry Office which had no cross and no officiating priest. One of the hammers that finally drove the nail of doom into our seemingly 'unholy' partnership echoed the repeated demands of the intrusive indigenes: "Why do you chaps not attend church? Why weren't you married in church?" And getting no satisfactory answer, the foundations of suspicion of a marriage contracted in hell, officiated by the devil of English perversion, were laid, presently growing into a formidable edifice of native cynicism. So at the very, very end, in a quest to break the religious tension coiled like a spring within him, I yielded to pressure – and to guilt – and resumed Catholic Church attendance, joining the throng of weekly Sunday congregants who not only felt obliged to worship but had to be *seen* to be worshipping. For me there was, at last, a new glorious refinement through the Englishman's expansive imagination. Here was the Englishman's desire to perfect virtually every pleasurable indulgence into a fine art. "After silence," observed Aldous Huxley, "that which comes nearest to expressing the inexpressible is music."

The one great difference now between Yours Truly and the English 'naturalists' whose aestheticism he has inherited is his unflagging duty to praise Almighty God directly, by name, for the wondrous glories of His handiwork emblazoned across the universe, while his English counterpart has long abandoned the identification of any divine artist behind the beautiful objects of creativity. This is in keeping with my newfound sanctuary, the Catholic Church, a place in which to dry the tears of broken love, and to replace the tears of readjustment with the tears wrought by the bliss of songs of praise.

However, many of my fellow natives appeared to recognise an element of 'offensiveness' in my new-found inspiration in worship, punctuated by my inclination to marvel at the innate beauty with which my fatherland is so exceedingly endowed, as English tourists were wont to do. "Look at the magnificence of those undulating hills!" I would cry out with an eloquent sweep of the hand. My native companions would quietly nudge each other in an unspoken sign that well summarised their view of their newly-returned compatriots – "Madness is just around the corner."

Another time Yours Truly would exclaim at the dizzying wonder of the glory flamed across the western sky by the burnished rays of the setting sun. "It's like the face of heaven!" And through some system of hydraulic pressure which we cannot explain, I would force a supply of tears to my eyes. "It's like the face of heaven!" I cried out again, "so fraught with the solemn mysteries of life and death, so untroubled and clear, so reassuring to the heart, because it's so tender and so beautiful. Can you chaps not feel all this?"

"Oh boy, trouble, serious trouble," my concerned pals would whisper to each other. "What's with the sunset, for heaven's sake?"

"And look at that lovely silhouette of tree-leaves fluttering in the breeze against the blueness of an expansive sky," I go on, "incredible in its mystic glory, uplifting in its spiritual flight of fancy, an eloquent testimony to the matrimonial bliss between heaven and earth. Too good for words, right?"

I turn to my companions, who nod in a show of diplomatic accordance that only serves to betray the eloquent but unspoken derision: "It is your sanity that has taken a spiritual flight of fancy, sir."

Demonstrating a stubborn insensitivity to the true feelings of his unlettered compatriots, I do not let up. "Now take the grave beauty of the drifting clouds in those uplifting skies, set in mysterious motion by a force that can neither be seen, felt nor heard. Don't you think it is wonderfully mysterious?"

The listening female relations can barely conceal their giggles.

"And moooooo to you, too, you uppity so and so!" I cry in exasperation. In my mind's eye I summon a large crowd of my bemused countrymen, and declare in rage, "Yes, I know where you think my next port of call will be and should be: wandering around the markets babbling incoherent nonsense, searching through trash-bins, and then on to the lunatic asylum as my final destination. It is you, and not I, who are misguided. It is for you, and not me or the white man, to remove the small coin before the eye that is hiding all else from sight. Why is the aboriginal African unable to appreciate God's handiwork and acknowledge it in words of worship and praise even outside the church? Must our vampire-like dash for material glory, as solid and deep as buildings with no foundations, obscure our duty to recognize and marvel in awe at, say, the innate beauty of creepers and vines covered in flowers; great towering ferns that exceed twelve feet in height; mammoth two-hundred-foot trees of a buttressed forest with a vastness of tangled roots; huge butterflies that shimmer in diverse hypnotic colours as they prance in the elusive dignity of their flight; black and yellow weaver birds plaiting their nests in trees; the enchantment of hornbills' whirring wings as they flap fast in their flight overhead, the fascination of their acrobatics as they soar and then plunge in the sky, their songs echoing in carefree abandon; the incredible flight of the swallow or hawk, like the speed of light; the spell of flamingos in flight in the sunset; the incandescence of a fish-eagle's white head in the sunshine as it sits high in the trees; the aesthetic perfection of an orchard; the snow-capped mountains? Have you accidentally interrupted the heart-throbbing song of a wren on a dreamy afternoon with the strains of Orpheus' *Can Can*, and then heard the compromise of the rejected fowl, so eager to please, begin to repeat the glorious *allegro* of those strains? Have you listened to the crash of formidable ocean breakers in a tempestuous storm? Have you stood on your balcony and hearkened to the rumba music of the wind, with the branches rustling in a frenzied 'limbo' dance? Do you not marvel at the kaleidoscope of greens of the countryside; the troops of monkeys that flee at your approach, scamper up into the trees, and from those sanctuaries continue to hurl fruits which, when any of them strike your person, will send the entire troupe into peals of squealing laughter? Have you not spent dreamy hours scanning the vast stretch of open sky from one distant horizon to another amid varying shades of blue ostensibly provided by interjecting peaks of hills and jagged mountain ranges? Does the predatory nature of the python deny our appreciation of the beauty of its geometric patterns?

"What terrifies one about beauty is the impossibility of exaggerating it. Its monstrous glories, infinite in number, are rooted in the intangibility of its magic and all-surpassing power. In its continuing elusiveness lies its enduring allure, for one is now confronted with the very source, the very ultimate, of beauty itself – the idea of God. And now you know that beauty is terrible, because no one can own it, because it is not just an idea but a monstrous reality that goes beyond anything we know or can fathom. 'There is no man who can see my face and live,' said the Holy Book.

"Why is it only the European who can immediately recognise and name the great trees of Africa, and the beasts of the field, the fowls of the sky, and the fishes of the sea with great appreciation and unfaltering accuracy? Why can we not recognize the poetry in a leaping impala or a galloping horse; the magic and fascination of well-arranged flowers; the unique brooding personality of an African storm, as though a savage expression of God's wrath? These are all elements of beauty, beauty to which we display ignorance at our peril, for, if you are blind to beauty, there is left in the wake of that blindness a basic residue of primitive paganism limited to the worship of the diabolical as our only effective source of power, making us expendable pawns in the hands of the Old Serpent. Hence not to fear God is the beginning of foolishness, and we cannot remain fools forever. So, as we tread the path of life, let our eyes be fixed up at the sky, where our Maker's handiwork is emblazoned across the heavens for the discerning disciple of our Lord and Saviour to drink in. That will afford us far greater vision than if we were staring ahead at the eyesore of human existence. That way, in fact, the blind would see, the deaf would hear, the dumb would speak, and the insane would become sane again. Hence talk to a woman and think of God – not the other way round; that way you would speak in tongues, and make sense – than if you were speaking to God and thinking of a woman.

"That was how the Englishman rose to the pinnacle. He started by fearing God through its Extraction – a.k.a 'Only Begotten'. He studied and treasured each of the countless creatures of Divinity which beautified the Earth, singing songs of praise, mouthing words of worship. As a result he developed a keener sight for the physical worth of all those inanimate objects, and utilized them. Look at all those diamonds, silver, gold, precious stones; he beheld them in their original rocky, uncut status, and understood that they had not been created for nothing, but for specific and definitive purposes. Likewise when our folks here in Africa trod down the hillsides to fetch water from the stream, the hard black rock that was the bed of the water in some parts was to them as meaningless as the smooth sandy soil and soft gravel to which they displayed a bat's eye in ignorance. But the English came, saw this rock, and from it created the coal that became a precious source of energy and power that replaced the cheap coal of England.

"Unhappily these English people, having travelled a negligible distance in the challenge of trying to replicate heaven here on earth, decided that they knew too much, and jettisoned the living God in favour of their science. The idea of a living God, or Christ, is fast being relegated to the status of fable. This radical rejection of God in favour of charting man's own destiny is the scourge of Western civilization today. So let us learn from their mistakes as we watch their plunge from the pinnacle. In our comparatively rudimentary status in the affairs of men, let us never lose touch with the source and giver of life. When next you see a fellow native who has been accorded the privilege of exposure, and in turn exalts in the wondrous products of God's handiwork, don't laugh at him; he is not mad."

The attendant crowd, duly provoked, is not allowed to disperse before a nun in its midst draws universal attention with the cry, "An observation please!" Complete with wire spectacles and a venerable aura, she cuts the picture of a lady scorned and bent on letting hell know no greater fury. "This affront of yours, sir, of our not being worthy of God's complete love, what's with the European's achievements anyway? What is new about any of them? Have you not heard the preacher Ecclesiastes" – and she begins to recite – "'the thing that hath been, it is that which shall be; and that which is done is that which shall be done: and there is no new thing under the sun... Is there any thing whereof it may be said, See, this is new? It hath been already of old time, which was before us. There is no remembrance of things that are to come with those which shall come after...' The intelligence ratio of every succeeding generation does not change significantly; what does change is intellectualization – which has nothing to do with intelligence.

"Hell, sir, modern exploration in this so-called space age continues to fail with the one all-decisive aggregate message from every astronaut upon his return to earth: 'I ain't see nuthin'!' Hell, these chaps haven't even started to sort out human problems here on earth before trying to discover heaven-knows-what up there. We've already been told that for now intelligent life is confined to two places in the universe – Heaven and Earth. If as much money as has been spent in space exploration was expended on improving human relations here on earth, we would have made more constructive discoveries that would have improved man's diminishing relationship with his Maker. Look at the fiasco and loss that visited this misguided idea of gender and racial harmony by sending astronauts of varying hue and both sexes into space in the recent past. Sure they roared up there, but left their lives behind, while the debris of their doomed craft was scattered by the four winds of heaven into oblivion.

"Likewise the Europeans build cars, and many lives are lost in them; they create the wonder of planes, and many fly to their deaths; they build trains, and many lives are taken when they derail. Where is the perfection that should come in the wake of such imaginative flair? You play God thinking you will create a heaven on earth, only to send millions of people to hell instead. Yes, we are backward, we cannot create, but rather than lose one life, I would rather not create technology. We will make do at our own snail's pace; we will get there in our own time – which is God's time – which is the best. Good night."

Yours Truly is impressed by this projection of cold logic, but is not wholly converted. He remains satisfied that for every emotional nun who would like to compromise painful truth, there are a thousand less religious and less philosophical mortals who will hanker to be a part of the inventive wonders of Western civilization.

In the final analysis, this scheme of things remains – for now – the world order of Western civilization, even if it will pass away in due time. Short of committing suicide in order to effectively reject it, one is of a duty to make the best of its benefits on offer before one receives his summons from above in the relatively short time availed to one – applying the niceties of good sense, good judgement, maturity and conscientiousness in so doing.

CHAPTER 11

The Eton Wall Game

I am satisfied that it would take the combined literary efforts of Shakespeare, Dickens and Shaw to perfectly capture a vivid picture of the life of my people, on home soil, through the eyes of a 'thoroughbred' Afro-Saxon for a well-digested appreciation by the casual observer offshore. There is so much at odds with the niceties of logic and deduction in such a challenge that it is difficult to know where to begin.

A succinct interpretation of the challenge was provided by Gurbaksh Chahal's sagacity when he observed: "The human body can stand almost anything. It's your mind that you have to convince." This apparent truism would seem to be compounded, in the African's case, by the opposing view of an Irish missionary, Rev. (Dr.) G.T. Basden, during his evangelistic duties in Nigeria in the early 1920s. As he saw it: "...the longer one lives amongst West African natives, the more one is convinced that it is a practical impossibility for the European to comprehend fully the subtleties of the native character... Let not this be thought strange, for the black man himself does not know his own mind. He does the most extraordinary things, and cannot explain why he does them. He is not controlled by logic: he is the victim of circumstance, and his policy is largely one of drift."

While this observation might have had some element of validity in those days, it fails to take into consideration the marked absence of two hundred years of industrial experience which helped to refine the developed nations. But the venerable missionary is on point in his subsequent observation that "This subliminal consciousness, by which all his movements are controlled, becomes practically a sixth sense. It is inexpressible in words but extremely powerful in action."

The situation as it prevails in the modern era is of a people who, well recognising their handicap in educational, scientific and technical progress, have nevertheless understood that they were created to *survive* – whatever the odds; and in the realm of the creative flair which developed the West, they had to demonstrate – and did demonstrate – an attitude of mind that regarded the faculty of logic as the art of going wrong with confidence! This brings into awesome reality Basden's observation of the people's status as being "practically a sixth sense... inexpressible in words, but, nevertheless, extremely powerful in action".

That "powerful" element is comparable to an army of marauders on a single-lane convergence, going with horrendous aggression to enforce its own inimitable rules of engagement, bowling over and trampling underfoot any impediment to its mission to record fees. It combines the extremes of sheer devilry of the Russian Roulette genre, on a corner-cutting fast-lane of scam, sleaze and criminal dexterity.

The final outcome, calculated on a global scale of entrepreneurship, represents a tribute to individual initiative captured in the motto of Britain's Special Air Service (SAS), 'Who Dares Wins'. The idea behind the motto is that if one has the courage and audacity to take risks, one will succeed in life, also interpreted to mean that courage is its own reward. The fallout for the hordes of Western entrepreneurs converging on the Nigerian capital to try to infiltrate the stifling officialdom of Central Bank to release massive funds owed for services rendered was reflected in the public cry of exasperation from a European Diplomat, "Nigeria is the world's nightmare!"

It is a striking fact that in 1717 Eton originated a famous sport called the Wall Game. It is still played there on a strip of ground 5 metres wide and 110 metres long next to a slightly curved brick wall. It is indeed a rough-tough sport not unlike rugby, the only major difference being the limitation of space for play in contrast to the football-pitch space available to the opposing rugby teams. Such limitation favours only the toughest, the strongest and the most durable of the players.

The game is essentially formed next to the wall, and crabs slowly against the wall until the ball emerges underfoot in the monumental heaving and pushing and grunting. Many players, especially those whose position is actually against the Wall, lose the skin off their elbows, hips and knees. A significant number have suffered varying degrees of bruises and cuts in the raucous scrummage, with at least one fatality recorded in recent years of a Nigerian pupil who was suffocated at the bottom of the scrum. That was fourteen-year old Tedum Saro-Wiwa, son of the celebrated environmental activist and poet Ken Saro-Wiwa (of blessed memory).

By a quirk of coincidence this game represents an eloquent instinctive survival pattern adopted by the generality of the people in Yours Truly's African environment to make up for their educational shortcomings. Notwithstanding the vastness of the space availed to its teeming population (4½ times the size of the British Isles), its awesome entrepreneurial spirit is limited by a wall of maladministration that finds its cause in the anomalies of its developing Third-World status. Hence, presented on a larger stage of true-life reality, the rules of survival are deadlier than any wall game or rugby ever dreamt of; and they are deadlier and more intimidating because those rules, by whatever name, were drawn up by Satan. Hence in the halls of justice, the only justice is in the halls.

Listen to the typical stoic defence of a fiercely patriotic citizen who lives and breathes the system, and such undaunted attitude permeates every branch of human endeavour in the private sector and in the polity:

"Were we created just to come and admire the bright lights of Western civilization? Is government your father's personal property? Should a sharp person not make more opportunities that he finds? Can I make my opportunities accord with the opportunities of people whose incomes are a hundred times mine? Why shouldn't I multiply my fortunes with that a hundred times if I can find the short cut to do it? Occasions are rare, and those who know how to seize them are rarer. Why shouldn't I be among the rarer? Should I cringe and cry 'God help me' because I am considered Third World? Am I not entitled to seek every avenue I can find to breathe in fresh air? Please don't talk to me about ethics. Grub first, *then* ethics!"

Hence, if the official figure for a government payroll is, say, 100, it will be 'refined' and multiplied unofficially to 200. 100 'ghost workers' will find themselves favoured in the payroll!

Nigeria's population, representing one in five of all the black people on earth, was intoxicated by an unspoken but prevailing rule to go in and slug it out. This resolve was rooted in its inability to compete on a national basis with the developed societies. So the challenge is viewed as an individual fight as opposed to patriotic duty; it has to be man-to-man, eyeball-to-eyeball, in the scrummage of rugby or the Wall Game, and may the best man win.

The African's policy is all about outwitting the system, outsmarting his fellow man, out-manoeuvring and out-fighting every legal obstacle placed in his path, and deftly slipping away with the spoils. The most sacrilegious sin that would be perpetrated in the circumstances is the '11th Commandment': Thou shalt not get caught! Hence you will see half-mile motorcades of successful political gladiators who started life as upstarts, climbed up the rungs with their wits, installed their impoverished relations and in-laws in key positions in the corridors of power, built mansions in their native village communities from their amassed millions, now being hailed by crowds that line the sides of the road to accord them a Messianic welcome. Let the petty thief who is able to nick an item of grocery from the market be unlucky enough to get caught in the act, and he will be lynched on the spot by an irate mob.

The population of overnight millionaires and billionaires, from office clerks to errand boys in the corridors of power, from cops, soldiers and other branches of law enforcement (including the Bar and the Bench), from every sector of human endeavour – even the bedraggled actors of 'Begging Incorporated' sitting by the dusty, unpaved waysides pitifully bleating their woes of blindness, deafness, hunger, physical handicaps, gesticulating their dumbness. These latter victims of fate, or so it would appear, melt away as if by magic at the onset of dusk, fit as fiddles, to divest themselves of the torn rags of deception and count their takings, and laugh all the way to the bank the next day. These artful patrons of survival merely stretch the elasticity of the nation's limitless wealth, because the flow of oil is believed to be limitless, with no official deadline set for its duration as a commodity.

What the stampede on the fast lane to have a sip of that lucrative oil has achieved endlessly is to rock the nation to its weary old foundations. The speed of structural development through sharp corner-cutting strategies, both by government and the private sector, is a marvel to behold, a tribute to sheer ingenuity. The rules of the game *dare* you ever to call it corruption! Look, listen and say nothing. Rather – try your luck and join the scrum. And all this superhuman energy in the murderous African heat that saps every fibre of one's being right from bone through to marrow! This is a monument to stamina from a higher world. But that is to be expected and taken for granted, for is it not glorious solar energy that consecrated them with blackness at the beginning of human civilization? The black man, then, could be said to be impervious to sunstroke. Not so his white counterpart, many of whom I saw faint in Britain, and perhaps many more collapse from sunstroke in my African environment since my homecoming.

In the light of the foregoing picture of the stampede to defy all odds and hit that big time, can it really be said that "the black man himself does not know his own mind"? One should learn to appreciate that concept as a variety of farce. But having said that, it is a striking fact that the casualties and fatalities from that scrum, from that fast lane – surpassed only by those "who dare not", are too many to be counted.

The fallouts from that scrum do not present an overall favourable image of my dear native land as a whole, and are collectively attracting bad press worldwide. I do not like to witness the drama created by an irate African-American guest at a hotel restaurant when he calls out to the waiter, "Hey man, I told you to bring me a bitter lemon and you doggone bring me a fucking beer. I guess you guys just aren't ready for independence."

The waiter shrugs (being African), takes away the beer, and returns later with a bitter lemon.

I can understand both sides of the drama. The African-American has been inspired, like so many descendants of the slave trade, by the fashionable 'back to Africa' concept being chanted with pride as back-up to the efflorescent image of themselves as 'Black is Beautiful, Black and Proud'. The reality that it is something of an illusion hits this young man like a punch to the jaw on coming to the acclaimed 'Giant of Africa' that Nigeria personifies in the world public gaze purely on the strength of oil wealth – only to encounter something of the reverse, certainly anything but the rosy romantic images that boost the Black American 'dream' back home. He has come and seen, for the most part, an attitude of mind a thousand years away in time engaged in a stampede for wealth – yet, as a nation, moving at snail's pace in the name of progress.

For the waiter being shouted at, his shrug is his eloquent apology for a situation that he cannot really help. He is a beneficiary of the nepotism that has placed him in a job for which he has undergone only the rudiments of proper training. And he fails to meet up, not because he is inferior to anybody, but because he is driven by a mind-set that says this job, this opportunity, is a stepping-stone to bigger things ahead – for which he must move faster than his shadow to accumulate. Hence he spends even his working hours dreaming and scheming, and pays scant attention to his duties in the five-star hotel dining-room. The actual job itself is more of a distraction outside of his salary.

I have had several opportunities to apply a more understanding approach, the most memorable being, "Waiter, please come and taste this pepper soup you've just served me."

"Any problem, sir?"

"Yes, there is a problem. Just taste it, that's all."

"Sir, you've always been a good customer. If there is anything wrong with the soup, we can take it away and serve you another one."

My features are now arranged for war. "Look, my friend, if you don't taste this pepper soup *now*, the whole world will hear what I'm going to say to you. Now taste this soup!"

"Okay, sir. Er... where is the spoon?"

"aHAA!"

The waiter, suddenly smitten with realisation, shrugs and goes to bring a spoon.

Other guests are not prepared to demonstrate my tolerance and understanding. I witness another guest snarl at the waiter, who, thanks to a very convenient absence of memory, has forgotten to bring the change, "Go and bring my change or else I will pour this beer in your face now."

Two dissatisfied African-American customers in another hotel grimace as they take their leave, one declaring, "Hey, man, I'm out of here. These people are full of shit!"

The mortal offender is a portly middle-aged waiter, who merely shrugs as he goes to serve Yours Truly – who happens not to be in the most agreeable frame of mind. Somehow he feels provoked by the waiter's indifference to the Afro-American visitors.

"Well, did you hear that?" Yours Truly challenges him. "He says you're full of shit. Why should that be?"

The waiter shrugs again and mutters something like, "I don't know their trouble."

Yours Truly wades in more forcefully. "Are you aware that those chaps are descended from the slaves, some of whom we sold to America as inferior beings, and now they're back here more advanced than we can ever dream of becoming?"

"Wonderful!" he exclaims in a burlesque of disbelief, clearly for want of something better to say.

"Yes, so try and give them better service so that they will not return to America and tell their people that those Africans are backward animals."

"Yessah!" he answers in meek deference, lacking the aptitude to offer even token defence.

These chaps will carry out their characteristic shrug as a way of token acknowledgement of their folly, but one will only hear "Sorry" if it is a more compelling situation, as when a careless driver rams into another car while dreaming of becoming super-rich and is confronted by the irate owner. A thunderous slap to his face sends him down on his knees begging for mercy and forgiveness; not that he is so much intimidated by the act of violence as horror at the prospect of having to fork out some of the fruits of his life's cherished sweat to pay for the damage. It is, at any rate, the kind of slap which I often wish could be delivered to every other dreamer living life upside down at the expense of the nerves of the more enlightened citizen.

The slap is the more desirable application of violence in these parts, more cultural than modern. History records that the black man south of the Sahara and his descendants had to be taught to bunch his hand into a fist and hurl it forcefully in a style that became known as 'boxing', and ultimately became the best in the world at it. So, as if making up for lost time, more fisticuffs in the streets can be witnessed every other day than all the punches thrown in the fifteen rounds of World Boxing Championship match. They draw crowds of obstreperous thrill-seekers, a few of whom will make efforts to intervene if the brawl threatens to get out of hand.

Draw the attention of the traffic cop engaged in directing the traffic and say, "Look, they're killing each other over there." The officer, distracted from his chore, raises a brief eyebrow and then answers dismissively, "Let them kill themselves," and continues with his mechanical direction of haphazard traffic. One has to spare a thought for the poor fellow, standing in the punishing heat all day long trying to control drivers who have not enjoyed the benefit of learning to drive with the British School of Motoring. Once in a while one comes across one of these law enforcement officers flaked out on his back on the lawn bordering the road, to the amusement of passers-by and vehicle passengers. But that could be seen only as a 'penalty' of law enforcement. The benefits are grand. For those eagle eyes miss no motoring offence, and the officer will extract his pound of flesh from the offender in lieu of incarceration in a stinking police cell. Policing is one of the most lucrative avenues for a quick and handsome profit.

One way or the other, there is profit all round for members of the citizenry seeking overnight prosperity. The bemusement of the resultant institutionalized chaos reaches a situation of pathos when extended to the airline industry, where the scandal of the overbooking of seats through the practice of bribery attracts extreme indignation. The moment the flight is announced there is a stampede as the passengers scramble to be the first in the queue before the mobile air-stair, and there are echoes of the Wall Game in the pushing, shoving and vociferous claims to positions. Further pandemonium resounds inside the aircraft as passengers present sundry boarding passes with the same seat numbers, with the passenger in the disputed seat also furnishing his own 'legitimate' pass for the same seat. It ultimately degenerates into another re-enactment of the Wall Game inside the cabin, with hoarse cries of defiance against the repeated order to leave the plane. "Let us all die here!"

Once in a while flight attendants and security personnel are unable to restore order at all, and the flight is cancelled. I once had to spend the night on a seat in the Departure Lounge amid the incessant whining of mosquitoes.

CHAPTER 12

The old boy network

The Second World War, it is said, was won on the playing fields of Eton (the school merely records that a substantial number of Eton-educated military officers served His Majesty's Government in the battle against Hitler). Africa south of the Sahara, with its special cultural circumstances, was not spared a lesser onslaught by virtue of its colonial past and the painful throes of transition in which it has since been enmeshed. From the information gathered in the preceding pages, it has indeed been a real war of survival – with no Geneva Convention to guide the tactics employed to that end.

But in the wake of many lingering thoughts of those glorious days of peace and security in good old London, what could have been a more welcome development than the arrival of an old school contemporary on my shores and the feverish efforts he embarked on to seek me out? By a quirk of coincidence he makes contact the day before my scheduled business trip to Lagos. We sit in the lounge of a five-star hotel overlooking a lagoon and reminisce over beer and small chops. What has brought him here?

"I hear you're taking the publishing industry by storm," says he. It turns out he has shares in a Nigerian-based UK company, which has a well-established household name, and which is at its wit's end over the snail's pace with which Central Bank is treating its perfectly legitimate request to repatriate some of its profits to London. As a last desperate measure, the company hit on the bright idea of trying to 'transfer' a substantial sum of cash hidden in the possession of the crew of a European airliner, with the notion, obviously, that their 'whiteness' would assist in bypassing customs. The sum was a black market accumulation running into six figures in pounds sterling. Unhappily, they were caught and arrested.

This old school contemporary, who shall be identified fictitiously as Simon, was anxious to prevent a scandal of volcanic proportions that would have been disastrous to the British administration even in faraway London. He flew into to Nigeria with the conviction that I had powerful family connections which could pull strings and bring a merciful end to the matter without ruffling the water's surface.

When I learned of the sum involved, I proposed a way out which I would have used if I had been confronted with such a plight. It would have involved a trusted African proxy of high standing having a one-on-one with the chief of police. Simon said he was not favourably disposed to the idea. I answered that he would then have to be favourably disposed to the idea of a public scandal and possible imprisonment, which would do no one any good. Would I act as such a proxy, he asked? I was not favourably disposed to that idea, well knowing that I could be roped in as a suspect in the whole conspiracy. He knew who could do it and how one could go around it in the shortest possible time, but there was the matter of how much he could be paid for his troubles if he made it happen. He was assured he would be made happy.

The meeting ended there. The matter was quietly resolved. But I did not hear from Simon again, nor was I aware when he quietly slipped out of Nigeria and went back to his London sanctuary.

When next I visited London and telephoned Simon in the night, the answer was something of a gruff rebuke. "What are you doing ringing up at this time of night?" The conversation ended with his sigh, like one reluctantly sitting up on the bed, "Oh, you black bastard." I took this in jest, seen as a light-hearted reminder of the same words that had escaped through even his own lips back at school. We arranged to meet for lunch the following day at an elite club in Mayfair. "Be my guest," said he.

It was an appetising meal of scampi, tartare sauce and French fries, accompanied by fine mature wine of long bottling years. That was all I received as commission for services rendered. Reflecting on the matter thereafter, I was left with a bitter taste in my mouth. I wondered how it would have gone down, after digesting the enormity of the trouble at hand, if he had responded with the mild rebuke, "Oh, you white trash." Simon's gushing charm at the time was clearly predicated on the knowledge that he was now on my own turf and was vulnerable to any hostile action. Having now accomplished his mission, and being safely back on his own turf, power was now back in his hand – as eloquently demonstrated by his subtle slur on my colour.

It is a striking fact that the encounter caused me, probably for the first time in my life, to reflect at length on the vexed issue of colour prejudice since leaving the shores of England. Hitherto it had been regarded as a fact of life, a recognised evil that had to be condemned and fought in the strongest terms – along with other forms of prejudice that exposed man at his most savage and depraved. It exposed the irrational superficiality of the human outlook on life. It was not difficult to draw an inference that such a weakness could not possibly be attributed to man's Maker, but to errant man himself.

In the analysis of good and evil, I gave grudging preference to my home environment over ready-made Europe. I decided it was better to rule in hell, as it were, than to serve in the heaven of abased man.

But for the first time I found myself, now a committed Christian, asking my Maker *WHY*? I knew *WHAT*: that the black man's colour was the sole basis for the global odium the mere sight of him evoked from all other races, including those of varying hue. But why? What was the reason? What did we do? It was more of a lament, a cry of protest, an expression of outrage, than any expectation of being given a cogent reason from On High.

I let my embittered, haphazard thoughts travel to the various global ports of call where irrational prejudice against my people had reared its ugly head. I recalled that during the American slave trade, and even after, a popular sport was 'nigger hunting'. A bunch of white bigots of the Ku Klux Klan brigade, with nothing better to do, would go hunting for blacks, chase them, and shoot them dead. Sometimes they would lynch them and relish the thrill of watching them die slowly, wishing they could kill them a thousand times over. Why? What did we do?

I remember that bigot in the smash-hit movie *Half-Moon Street*. During a dinner party of all-white guests, two women were lamenting the population explosion in China. One was so appalled as to suggest that "they breed like rabbits", while the other claimed that their population had reached the one billion mark. Then this diminutive white geezer butts in to say, "You're both wrong: there are only two people in China. A billion is hardly a number in the true sense of the word.' 'So,' says the heroine, 'how many people are there, would you say, in Germany, for instance?' 'Four'. 'In Africa?' 'None.' Why? What did we do?

In the Angolan civil war, a murdering white mercenary called

Callan used innocent black Angolan villagers for target practice, just wasting them with shots to the head to test out new weapons. Why? What did we do?

In South Africa the other day, and this is long since apartheid was abolished, an enraged white farmer shot dead four of his black servants. He just could not control his abhorrence of the black African. Sure, he was given four life sentences. But, still, the question must be asked: What did we do to God that such extremes of brazen contempt, irrational prejudice and opprobrium – not shown even to the beasts of the field – can be visited on blackness, most notably African blackness?

Arabs used to castrate black slaves to obviate the so-called abomination of a black man having carnal knowledge of an Arab woman. That is why one hardly sees marriage or cohabitation between black men and Arab women. Why? What did we do? What is it about our blackness that so contaminates the rest of the world? How can a government create a law – the apartheid law – that segregates a whole group of people simply because their skin is black? Why? What did we do?

Then I remember that American Mafia hit-man called Joey, who wrote his memoirs as a professional murderer. He talked about blacks in crime – the very area of human endeavour in which we are said to be notorious and proficient. Even in that he said that blacks had always been subservient. He said that while everyone else was fighting and organising and establishing their own system, blacks weren't doing a goddam thing. He was asked why there was so much prejudice against blacks, and said, "I really don't know". There you are, you see. It's irrational prejudice. Then that killer added, "Maybe it's felt that down through the years they always bitched and belly-ached about what they didn't have, but they never actually tried to do anything about changing things. Years ago the opportunity was there up in Harlem, but the blacks did nothing about it." And that is true, in a way. The same is applicable to every white administration taken over by blacks. The whites build the institutions, and invariably we turn them into ghettoes. We don't seem to be able to maintain or manage anything on our own without significant white presence.

Then there was that U.S. marine in the movie *Tears of the Sun* who was sent to evacuate a white female professor of medicine from the volatile Niger-Delta jungle. He growled cynically to one of the lamenting evacuees, "God left Africa a long time ago." Why? What did we do?

Then let us remember that U.N. peacekeeping general in the movie *Hotel Rwanda*. The massacre of Tutsis was in progress. The general thought the French army buses coming to evacuate people trapped in the fighting would also take Rwandan refugees, but the first thing the French colonel in charge told the general was, "No Rwandans!" The shocked general goes to accept a drink from the Hutu manager of the hotel where he has been putting up, whose wife is Tutsi. He tells the manager, "You should spit in my face. Those guys in Washington couldn't give a cuss about you. It isn't just that you're niggers: you're Africans."

These memories flooded my mind after my unsatisfactory encounter with Simon. The dust settled with two policies that I pledged myself to pursue: (1) a deeper understanding, tolerance and compassion for the failing of my underprivileged countrymen in their tortuous efforts to build a modern nation: and (2) to embark on painstaking research into human history in a quest to unlock the mystery behind the endless oppression of the genus black in this scheme of things – buoyed in this resolve by a statement I had read that was credited to Napoleon Bonaparte: "History is a set of lies agreed upon."

I had never felt a greater sense of belonging in my African environment than in the wake of my experience with the aforesaid Simon. I was left feeling vindicated by my strong conviction, long held since leaving my revered *alma mater*, that there was no way the Aryan/Caucasian could consider the black man to be his equal – except before God.

Pursuant to the proposed research, I embarked on a 15-year study of the Holy Bible from cover to cover, three good times, spending an appreciable number of years in the intervening period in a determined quest to understand the subtle shades of meaning inherent in Allegory as the language of the Living God and Parables as the language of His extraction, Christ. At the end of the day, I felt fulfilled, able to view the world in a very different light from previously – in that Napoleon was indeed vindicated by the truism that much of human history, as taught in the Western educational system, was presented through false and biased concepts. It laid bare the deceptions upon which the wheels of civilized modern-day global thinking revolve.

I became unperturbed and philosophical, but no less stressed, by the rigours of Third World existence, having again recognised one all-important truism: that this scheme of things was ruled by Western civilisation. Accordingly, the West calls the shots. Like other civilisations before it, it will pass away one day, but in the interim it is for my fellow people to endeavour to pursue a policy of continuous improvement from what is available, and make the best of what is on offer by sheer individual initiative fired by inventive power and creative drive. Uncountable numbers have been able to hit the big time in this manner, especially descendants of the Western slave-trade offshore, and many home-based Africans – especially the people of Nigeria, who have the largest population of Western-trained manpower south of the Sahara.

CHAPTER 13

The scourge of the Been-Tos

I am peeved by my people's painful gullibility, which closes their eyes to the reality that the 'seeing is believing' aphorism does not explain their perceived inferiority to other groups of people because of skin colour. Their shortcomings in life stem from circumstances and climatic conditions, as opposed to any conferment of inherent inferiority by man's Maker. But a part of my agony has been wondering how to convert them all to the truth of a deliberate policy of brainwashing calculated to line the nest of their former colonial powers. How do I he explain to them, for instance, that their own power has to be tilled from the lucrative soil of their countryside and not sapped by the concentration camps of the cities?

When my people approach me with wide, expectant eyes to hear tales of wonder about Great Britain, how do I explain that the greatest piece of enlightenment that the West bestowed upon me was the actual discovery of Mother Africa? Reflect on the full meaning of this: I had to travel to Great Britain to find out who I was and appreciate the worth of Africa. How then do I explain to my people that by virtue of this discovery, I have little more to offer them from England than they already possess, but they have yet to realise it?

If mere words could provide the remedy, then it would have been easy to explain to my people that they went wrong initially by falling into a dream-world – by believing that they could possess overnight the technological marvels that it took the white people centuries to develop and enjoy. They failed to consider the circumstances that had rewarded Westerners with these wonders – the Arctic temperatures that compelled them to explore and create for their very survival, that called for the right attitudes, dedication, foresight and imaginative power, so that every discovery, every invention, needed to be practised endlessly until it was honed into a fine art and could become an intrinsic part of their raison d'être. And make no mistake about it – many, very many, lives were lost in the formidable challenges thrown up by the discovery process. It was never a bowl of cherries – until the very end, until the recession of the waves after the terrible tsunami.

Hence the African's climatic conditions were not designed to inspire the indigenous people with the inherent 'get up and go' that would have blessed them in similar manner. On the contrary, the heat instilled lethargy, atrophy, shaping the people into physically-oriented creatures, to the end of exposing them to the deceptive miscalculation of the 'seeing is believing' illusion. In consequence every item of technology dangled by the white explorer held in its power the converting mesmerism that spelled the beginning of the African's troubles, the initial devaluing of his culture. A frenzied rush shook the African homeland as its people trooped over to England to receive the benefits of this new way of life from their source. Whole African villages competed against each other, squandering their entire resources, in order to send their most talented children to master the English language and scoop English degrees, with the expectation that they would return one day to create in their traditional communities the same technological wonders that bless the homes of the white geniuses. These 'Been-Tos' come home after many years to great rejoicing from their less-privileged folks, adorned in fancy Western-style clothes that testified to the 'civilisation' process that they have experienced across the seas, speaking in a cacophony of English and flashing credentials that proclaimed the degrees for various branches of education and technical know-how.

But something went wrong. After a long and tortuous spell of watching and waiting, the unlettered indigenes observed that the benefits which they had almost starved to pay for had shown little signs of coming forth. What they did not know, and could not be expected to know, was that one fundamental element was missing from the brilliant achievements of these Been-Tos during their academic career in England: an element that, in effect, overshadowed all their achievements and without which those ambitious students had been a total dead-loss to Africa, and the precious money spent on them a complete waste. They lacked the correct attitudes. If the same patriotic attitudes employed by the white man to achieve industrial success were adopted by the African Been-To bent on acquiring his secrets, a cultural revolution would long since have taken place in Africa. The continent would by now have become a financial and military force to be reckoned with, a model of stability; and if the stiff-necks of the Dutch Reformed Church worshipping the Almighty in the name of apartheid had not been removed from down south of the African homeland, then that system would at least have collapsed by their very fear of the black man's own capabilities and solidarity.

But the wrong attitudes were applied. To start with, the wretched indigenes found that the Been-To had not come home with the intention of sharing with them the benefits of their achievements abroad, but with the attitude that the villagers should now feather his nest for the rest of his life by virtue of his European exposure. His essential function, then, became that of a parasite – expensive, debilitating and deadly; and if one considers that we are talking of several generations of such Been-Tos, one has little need to wonder at the speed of the black African's economic self-suffocation.

On seeing that they are not going to benefit from their misplaced investments, the villagers in staggering numbers discard their pride and their culture to engage in a stampede – to pander to the hero-worship sought by these Been-Tos, in a bid to find some gateway to the opportunities and refinement of the Englishman's castle. In the light of this, it is not difficult to understand how such a little dot of an island, with coal its only natural resource, was able to create an empire which enabled her to tower to legendary heights of economic might, while Mother Africa, with all her vastness and uncountable natural resources, has till this day remained an economic ghetto, barely able to feed her children.

My disquiet over this unhappy state of affairs has been heightened by my people's penchant for invoking Handel with a chant of 'Hallelujah' at the homecoming of every degreed Been-To; and then, with the echo of our hosanna still ringing in the air, we complain in dismay when the Been-To fails to perform and our problems multiply instead of reducing. Does it really require Handel to turn in his grave with a dismissive wave of the hand before our people wake up to the idea that the degreed Been-To may *not* be Africa's Messiah? That the African problem will not be solved by the degreed Been-To because the degreed Been-To may be the *crux* of the problem?

There are two categories of these Been-Tos. There is the adult group, comprising those indigenes who leave home as grown-ups for a course in the West, returning after several years exactly the same people (by virtue of having travelled as adults and not as impressionable adolescents), but having discovered new avenues of guile in their course through which they will attempt to realise their get-rich-quick ambitions – to the detriment of their own people. Then there is the category of indigenes who undergo full Westernization as adolescents, ultimately to return home resolved to carve out for themselves an exclusive niche that will distinguish them as the cream of society.

Members of the former group have one thing in common – overnight wealth first and foremost, through whichever discipline they pursue. They recognise that they have not been equipped by nature to create for themselves the technological phenomena that bless the West, and quite likely – perish the thought! – will not achieve such creativity in their lifetime. So they will attempt to accumulate for themselves as many of those Western comforts as possible, establishing a European-style status in their society, and in that way running the risk of setting themselves up as agents for the European way of life.

The European spirit of self-sacrifice, which has remained an intrinsic feature of his continuing survival and solidarity, will not be invoked by these Been-Tos, who see the issue as a personal one: they have not had centuries of the industrial experience which would have invoked that spirit, nor the climatic conditions: they have had their share of suffering, and feel it is now their turn to prosper. Moreover, in appreciating that they cannot hope to compete against the eons of established craft of living mastered by the West, they accept that the areas of real opportunities open to them are confined to their African environments, with their British masters in the background officiating over the *Made in Britain* 'chess-game', waiting for the guaranteed checkmate that will be sapped from the African oil. Unhappily that is the business of profits and exploitation, patronised by both black and white alike when opportunities present themselves.

And in accordance with the 'follow the leader' policy, the less privileged masses will instinctively conform to the status quo, unable to grasp the consequences of, say, eating with British-made silver cutlery as opposed to their own home-made wooden implements. With wooden cutlery, they would be saving money at every consumption, because the sweat sapped by the creation of those spoons – when translated into money – would remain in their home. By being persuaded that the use of European silver cutlery is a mark of civilization while 'wooden' cutlery symbolises backwardness, they would in effect be subsiding the European economy at every meal.

When one reflects further that culture is not limited to gastronomical implements, that it involves every activity from birth to death, one observes that we are, in effect, existing to subsidise the European economy. Every individual, from the crawling infant to the hobbling old man, is adding to the purse of the European taxman for merely exercising his God-given right to breathe. Calculated in terms of our entire population paying tax to Britain (or any other European former colonising power), year after year, generation after generation, one need not add up the extent of the nation's losses to appreciate what an exorbitant 'merchandise' the English language has been to our folks.

And it is for this that uninformed indigenes throw lavish banquets to welcome the degreed Been-To as the golden asset of African society.

By rights the Been-To possesses the requisite attributes to steer the African 'ship' on a positive development course, a course that should long since have rewarded the African people with handsome dividends, had the goodwill been there from the outset. That they remain 'Third World' in the face of innumerable natural resources bestowed on their soil by Mother Nature owes its cause not to any divine decree of their perceived inferiority, but to the Been-Tos who have failed to deliver the goods.

We say glibly that our children and grandchildren will make up for the lost time that resultsed from our failures, yet fail to observe that in the absence of any conscious effort on our part to implant in their receptive minds an awareness of the marked departure they must make from this present trend of institutionalised maladministration, we must entertain clear visions of their abandoning ship with their own loot, having expedited the sinking process with the examples passed on to them by their predecessors.

These observations, coincidentally, constitute my line of thought one afternoon when I chanced to be the first in a queue of motorists, only for a goods-train driver to stop on the level crossing and settle down to conversation with his mate. It became quickly apparent that this action was none but bloody-mindedness, to demonstrate a warped sense of power to hold the world to ransom. My outraged challenge to him, amidst the protesting horns of the other motorists, was answered with a wink, a saucy grin, and the retort, "That's life." The chance appearance of two uniformed policemen on the beat during those heated moments sent him on his way.

Reflecting on that incident later, Yours Truly recognises the formidable task that will be involved in any official quest to revise such an attitude on a national scale; for it is by no means untypical. If it is not your train driver, it is your motorist on the road, your bank staff, your office worker, your clerk, your doctor, your nurse, your average politician – all possessed of this curious streak that demands their display of power with the mind to be create difficulties in order to be noticed.

On arriving at a hospital with a dying accident victim one evening, I was taken aback by the flippant dismissal of the nurse in charge: "Take him somewhere else, we are full up." As luck would have it, my father, now a retired Judge, was the Chairman of that Federal Government Hospital Board, and he used that advantageous position to intimidate the nurse and secure the desired change of heart on her part, together with apologetic gestures and excuses and prompt attention to the bloodied, unconscious patient.

On serious reflection later on, I wondered whether the nurse could really be blamed. While not excusing her initial callousness, it seems only realistic to recognise that she was merely following the examples set by those in the corridors of power. In consequence, such callousness has become virtually endemic in the make-up of the national character. What, for instance, gives a motoring offender the courage to ignore a police request to search the vehicle, and next moment to drive off with the policeman spread-eagled on the back of the speeding van in his determination to pursue this contempt of the law to the logical end? (At the end of the exercise he will be bought off with a bribe anyway.)What gives a State Police Commissioner the courage to repeatedly ignore a High Court summons to appear before the Judge? Who has the courage to go and apprehend him? What gives government office staff free rein to practise 'absenteeism' at will to engage in private business while collecting a government salary for doing damn all? What justification would there be to punish these misdemeanours, since 'the system' has left everyone under no illusion that with the national treasury all but emptied by the privileged clique at the helm of affairs, it is now every man for himself?

This unedifying picture lays bare the option embarked upon by the so-called leaders of the Been-To clique to seek a short-cut to stability through emulation of every aspect of creativity practised by Africa's former colonists. The curse of this copy-cat disposition reveals, as nothing else can, the absence of that all-important policy of *incentive* to motivate the people. I am pained by this deficiency, which permeates every branch of human endeavour. The system in developed societies works through the recognition of incentive as a goodwill gesture to bring out the best in the individual. With incentives, the individual is inspired to get up and go, to give his all, with dedication and loyalty to duty. With incentives, a nation becomes worth dying for. Without incentives, the people are compelled to grab what they can by hook or crook, and the nation stagnates.

In my Africa the nearest to this phenomenon is the practice of *dash* – which generates bad feeling for all concerned. It comprises unspoken extortion and blackmail to a level of do-or-die. For the most part the practice is structured and organised almost to a level of the Mafia, and when it involves the investigation of a citizen who is above suspicion, he has the unassailable power of denial, placing an insurmountable burden of proof upon the accuser. Add to such anomalies the affliction of the endless levies and taxes that have added to 'respiratory challenges', and the perennial non-payment of salaries to Government workers (at timges in arrears for several months), the negative faces of human nature will continue to dominate in the public gaze. Your train driver, then, will feel a need to inconvenience society; your nurse will feel no obligation to tend to the dying; the violent touts will not respect the uniformity of law enforcement; the government worker will not recognise he integrity of government.

I am of the conviction that if governors and private entrepreneurs were to adopt, for instance, a strategy which provides for a reduction in salaries for negative conduct, counterbalanced by healthy bonuses for good conduct, his motherland would begin to create the basis for a viable society. Such a strategy would have a moulding effect, which could only serve to attract dedication to duty; dedication would, in turn, give rise to good organisation, which would make room for progress and development; and with development would come stability.

With incentive as the ideal bait to attract goodwill and cooperation, the mistakes (or misdeeds) of those in power become less glaring, if scarcely noticeable by comparison to the present trend, and their sins more worthy of pardon. The Been-Tos, therefore, having been privileged (by the sweat of the people whom they aspire to lead) with the opportunity to master these secrets of progress from their Western counterparts, have now to fulfil their side of the social contract.

CHAPTER 14

Remembering great Been-Tos

In order to avoid possible embarrassment, the names of the couple being introduced here will be fictitious. Sharon, a middle-aged American health administrator of Caucasian extraction, married a Nigerian US-based radiographer in spite of what the neighbours might say. They had two children, and ultimately she followed him back to his Nigerian home. For a long time he had nursed a patriotic urge, after thirty years away from his people, to return home and use the benefit of his exposure in the West to contribute to the nation-building process in his fatherland.

The couple, well-to-do by US middle-class standards, have planned carefully, leaving behind a nice home with mortgage fully cleared and a handsome sum saved in the bank. The couple's towering professional status has been avidly recognised by the Nigerian government at Federal level. Sharon was appointed to the position of Deputy Administrator at a Federal Government Hospital, while her husband Joe headed the Department of Radiography in the same hospital. The couple were thus presented with a golden opportunity to change a classical Third-World system which, some would say, was mired in a jungle of sleaze described by a Military General in a *coup d'état* that would one day take over the affairs of state in the unedifying terms: "Our hospitals have been reduced to mere consulting clinics".

Nevertheless, in her innocence and unimpeachable integrity, Sharon gave her all in the conviction that her wide experience in hospital administration would contribute towards the development of her husband's home country. Unhappily, little could she realise, until it was too late, that she was fighting a losing battle, for she was against forces that had ostracised her even before she started. Her natural predilection for discipline, order and efficiency had put her at a distinct disadvantage even before she set out for these shores. Not even her husband, by virtue of his long-term sojourn in the West, could have envisaged his people's capacity for ruthless guile in the local system of profits and exploitation. It did seem, with the great feasts and hero worship showered on him, that Joe was considered indispensable to their needs on the sentimental scale of a long-lost son-of-the-soil and much-awaited Messiah.

In their innocence the couple failed to discern the subtle actions calculated to dispatch them back from where they had come. They were not expected to fully appreciate that these were a people not yet ready for honest leadership. The couple found themselves saddled in a hotel suite for months, unable to secure proper accommodation – contrary to what had normally prevailed for top-ranking Government functionaries. All the essential files that would have facilitated Sharon's work schedules developed k-legs and went AWOL (absent without leave) and proved exceptionally difficult to find.

Sharon, for her part, encountered considerable difficulty in her stressful efforts to obtain a residence permit. It necessitated innumerable trips to faraway Lagos, away from her work. In Lagos she was further frustrated by the institutionalised practice of *dash,* which was alien to her nature; and when the truth finally dawned through privileged information, she would not hear of it. In consequence, at every office to which she was directed she encountered the chronic delays, inefficiency and snail's pace action that characterised the African way of life.

Sharon and Joe aged years in a matter of months. It took some time before it dawned on her, even before it dawned on him, that her invaluable experience was not only not appreciated but actually presented a stumbling block to the corner-cutting aspirations of the get-rich-quick brigade under her authority. She understood that only through chaos, disorder and 'lost' files could Government funds be siphoned away to enlarge individual pockets and bank accounts, and huge salaries collected by 'ghost' workers.

It became clear to Sharon that her God-given approach to the creation of a near-perfect administration threatened to expose too many skeletons in too many cupboards, and to terminate a lucrative 'business'. And when she maintained an admirable tenacity in the face of all the subtle attempts to dislodge her, she was presented with chilling evidence of just how dangerous her uncompromising attitude was. Desperation set in among the criminals over whom she held sway. They resorted to drastic measures to bring about her physical removal without harming her directly: that would have attracted international outrage that would never have died down until those responsible were brought to justice.

Her husband Joe was targeted. Under cover of a dinner party in their honour at the same exclusive hotel where they lodged, he was the victim of food poisoning that almost took his life. That he survived could only be put down to a gracious act of Providence – much as his wife was able to deploy what influence she could wield to ensure he was given the best medical assistance available.

It required no stretch of the imagination to understand that this had been a calculated murder attempt, for with her husband out of the way, there would then be no reason for her continued presence in Nigeria.

Sharon started to panic – understandably so, as she could now appreciate the depths to which her enemies were ready to descend in order to see the back of her. Suddenly she wanted out, she wanted to return to the US. But her husband would not hear of it. He saw it as running away from a challenge, abandoning his people. So the first cracks started to appear in their matrimonial wall. Inclination and duty became locked in stalemate. They started to fall apart.

"Your society is rotten, Dillibe, rotten to the core," she lamented to me. "Your people don't want to progress. They revel in chaos so that they can hide their dubious carryings-on."

I was sympathetic, but though I applauded her courage and integrity, I could not bring myself to openly condemn my people, who needed understanding and tolerance as well as condemnation and punishment because of challenges that were peculiar to their country.

In spite of my gentle encouragement to stay on and get used to the system, she felt she had had enough. She and Joe fell apart, he in Nigeria, she and their two kids back home on her US home turf. It was a tragic break-up of a beautiful marriage. She remarried, to a fellow Caucasian in the US, and Joe married a Nigerian lady.

I recall that there was actually a period, in the recent history of post-independence Nigeria, when it became a source of entertainment to swap anecdotes about the scourge of being a Nigerian, but now those real-life horror-stories had ceased to amuse. One recalls those good old days in London when it was the fashion to condemn colour prejudice with the implied projection of black people as models of rectitude: now, settled in the harsh reality of home life, many Been-Tos are barely able to restrain ourselves from imploring the former colonists, "Please come back, all is forgiven."

After so much costly ground-shifting from one disastrous system to another, after watching their efforts to survive as a nation win and lose, my people are back to square one, in a limbo of unknowing.

If I was shocked by the horrors that afflicted Sharon and Joe, I felt open-mouthed disbelief at the unspeakable fate that befell some black heroes, celebrated back in London as respected leaders of the Black Power struggle, when they returned home to a true hero's welcome to start with, and were then sent to hell as converted villains in the wake of their human rights agitations against perceived 'primitive' power play.

A London-educated relation to Yours Truly, married to a West Indian lady from Barbados, suffered a fate no less hideous. They were both employed in respective leadership positions in Federal Government health agencies, both fiercely intolerant of corruption in any guise. One day they received a visit from armed robbers in the early hours. The three hoodlums carted away their expensive property and creature comforts in a two-hour operation that involved a veiled move to rape the wife, which was aborted for lack of time. The couple, unnerved by the experience, left Nigeria a few months later and re-settled in their former London base.

Salami Coker, another example, was a well-known Sierra Leonean London-based actor who enjoyed fair success in such award-winning films as *Born Free* and *Sinbad and the Eye of the Tiger*. Both movies recorded strong box office success, and were internationally distributed by Columbia Films. Additionally Salami did a lot of TV commercials, and acted in theatre roles. His status as one of the early actors from Sierra Leone was a great pride to his people, to Africans on the home continent, and to black people in the Diaspora. In spite of his small but well-muscled frame, he was exceptional in sports, triumphing as an athlete, a boxer and above all as a weightlifting champion.

Salami was also a formidable activist within the London Black Power Movement, and in that vein a fiery speaker at London's Hyde Park Speakers' Corner against colonialism in Africa in particular and white racism in general. His fiery temperament resulted in his beating up many white hecklers and opponents following heated altercations on race issues. Returning home to Sierra Leone in 1972, he hit the big time further after becoming the founding Director of Culture in the newly established Ministry of Culture and Tourism. Subsequently he became the PRO for a highly successful fishing company, Sierra Fisheries, owned by Sierra Leone's richest man at that time, Jamil Sahid Mohamed.

But those relatively unlettered Africans who were seeking fame and fortune in the quickest way possible did not take to being overshadowed by celebrated Been-Tos for any length of time. Salami's agitations for human rights and democratic principles, popular in the wake of his celebrated homecoming, made him secret enemies. Before he knew what was happening he was arrested at a palm-wine joint by operatives of the new military junta that took power in 1992. Within a few days of being locked up with a small group of other human rights activists, he was put into a Black Maria, taken to a remote location and shot at point blank range. There was no doubt that it was an extra-judicial killing.

I was horrified by this development, having been well-acquainted with Salami in London, but by the time of that tragedy he had come to recognise that the popular 'Back to Africa' concept among black people in the West had its risks for the homecoming African Been-

To. It had become abundantly clear that fame accrued from the struggles against white racism on its home source was expected, at the end of the day, to have exhausted its usefulness there on that same soil. The 'hosannas' the hero was welcomed with on coming back to his home roots was, at best, a nine-day wonder that would be relegated to yesterday's news, especially for those many indigenes bursting to go and sample that developed heaven they had heard so much about.

Obi Egbuna, a larger-than-life London-based Nigerian novelist, playwright and author of several hard-hitting books on race, almost met the same fate as Salami. A dear friend of mine, he had been published by some of Britain's leading book publishers – notably Oxford University Press, Fontana and McGibbon & Kee, with works across drama, fiction, short stories and current affairs. He was as fiery and combative as Salami Coker, assaulting several of his critics as Speakers' Corner, and was jailed for six months in London for masterminding a plot to kill British police officers. Understandably he was *persona non grata* with the British establishment for the inciting power of his anti-white rhetoric as the pioneer of the Black Power Movement, and survived an almost fatal assassination attempt by hired white killers which expedited his final departure from the shores of Britain in 1973.

The welcome that greeted his homecoming to Nigeria soon withered away when his excessive anti-West rhetoric began to grate on people's nerves, including those of members of his extended family. He began to encounter hostile challenges at speaking engagements, and ultimately attracted infamy from his close association with a state administrator who had been accused of building a personal estate from public funds. Obi's life remained in permanent danger from death threats. He carried a dagger for self-defence in the fearful anticipation of a physical attack at any moment. The insecurity he felt precipitated his flight from the shores of Nigeria, and he settled in the US in self-enforced exile, passing away in 2014 in Washington almost forgotten.

It became evident to me that the attitude of Western-based black people towards the vexed issue of colour prejudice is not altogether shared in the same extreme light by their people on the African continent. In Africa certainly there exists the awareness of the injustices perpetrated by the early colonists on account of colour, but those have been largely overshadowed by independence and the subsequent stampede to luxuriate in its spoils on home turf. Moreover, there was the added stimulus of sampling the niceties of the developed societies offshore.

The white man, then, personifying quality education and material wealth, remains eminently in demand; and the bright lights of his cities sparkle like clustered beacons of hope to which black Africans will always be attracted like moths. The hue and cry over colonialism and prejudice are gradually falling out of vogue, and the concept of 'black brotherhood' something of an anachronism, with scant followership in Africa, and with ethnic and factional dissent now taking the show in another facet of the dog-eat-dog system.

This reality seemed to become more blatant when I, in the role of a casual observer, acknowledged that almost all my fellow Nigerian intimates, friends and acquaintances during those London days, including close relations and distant ones, have gone off the radar with stress-related illnesses since coming home. Most of them were beneficiaries of polytechnic education, some postgraduate students, many avowed disciples of the notion that to properly address its own peculiar compelling challenges to create the basis for a viable society, Africa's Third-World environment required people educated to meet a specific need. To that end, technocrats were the answer.

Those fellow countrymen referred to above exuded supreme confidence that they could turn around the fortunes of their homeland. They were colourful, larger-than-life individuals sporting an aura of absolute control, such as to reassure the casual observer that they were equal to any challenge and could give Nigeria a medium-power status. They overshadowed their fellows at social gatherings, enunciated answers to every problem, and emerged the souls of reason in every argument. They personified real hope for our beleaguered motherland. Maybe, as a further boost to their ego, there was the remarkable camaraderie that bound them together in their alien English abode, as if they did indeed recognise the beauty and exigency of brotherhood in an environment that was not altogether amicably disposed to their presence in such large numbers. They did indeed personify birds of the same feather that flocked together – in parties or wedding receptions, in other social gatherings, one looking after the other's interests.

But when they returned home, praised and feted to high heaven, and were presented with the challenge of serving, before you knew it they were flattened by the raucous rugby scrum of Nigerian life. They lacked the drive, the endurance, the courage, the daring, the wits, the guile, and the sheer grit to fight to the finish, unable to accept the challenge of kill or be killed. One by one they dropped out of circulation, became ill, and went six feet under. They never imagined that it was easy to gather the thrill of ambition and courage in the ready-made paradise of London, where life was laid out on a golden trolley by comparison. But the nitty-gritty of being relocated to a 'jungle' atmosphere, amidst real-life dare-devils who demonstrated irrepressible superhuman energy, and operating with rules drawn up at a remote period in time, was truly terrifying.

This was eloquently analysed by the aforementioned Dr. G.T. Basden, who observed: "The will of the tribe or family, expressed or implied, permeates his whole being, and is the deciding factor in every detail of his life. It is a sort of intangible freemasonry; the essence of the primary instincts of the people. Men constantly act contrary to their better judgment, and, at times, even wrongly, because they firmly believe they have no alternative: they dare not oppose the wishes of the people. Consequently, though there may be independent thought, there is seldom independent action, probably never where other members of his tribe or family are involved, however remotely... He is under the influence of an atmosphere which emanates from the whole tribe."

These attitudes have not changed significantly since the 1920s era in which Basden conducted his missionary duties. The modern-day 'Been-To', on returning home finally, finds himself being inadvertently assimilated into this frame of mind, with the adoption of an approach to thinking problems that is impervious to reason. Before he knows it, the watertight camaraderie that existed with his fellow Been-Tos in Europe is gradually whittled away, dissipated by comparatively primitive attitudes if he is to survive and feel secure and protected amongst his people. He is drawn away from his old intimates by the 'primitive exactions' of uncompromising die-hard political power-play, sibling rivalry within extended family groups, factional dissension, and petty domestic squabbles that find their root many decades away in the past. Old intimates from Europe often become overnight foes, political rivals, do-or-die adversaries in the struggle for the plums of office.

At the end of the day it is a monumental drain of precious resources, physically and mentally exhausting and soul-destroying. Every other fellow man, stranger, foe, relation, cousin, brother, is distracted by the very sight of his happiness, his fresh, prosperous appearance, his receptiveness – which all go to suggest a quality of good life and happiness that has eluded his 'competitors'. Whereupon those self-appointed competitors start to scheme for his downfall, to create obstacles in his path, to present hurdles to his ambitions and to sully his good name to third parties. The more 'primitive' distant relations consult local shrines with the aim of bringing about his madness, calamitous misfortune or death.

This is the classic scenario in which the Been-To finds himself. As a result he will age prematurely and become increasingly weak, no longer possessing the willpower to continue to slug it out against unlettered daredevils in the survival game. Stress attacks his sanity, and he becomes a shadow of his previous larger-than-life personage. Even fresh air seems to have been privatised in the ensuing *mêlée*, and he is assailed with respiratory challenges.

I was traumatised by the tragic demises of dear friends who had seemed immune to the visitation of death and moved to tears on several occasions. The sense of gloom I felt sometimes was as if I had been left on my own, abandoned to face the overwhelming numbers of Satan's marauders. It was almost as if they had fled to the peace and sanctuary of death. I was even more horrified by the blatancy with which death was dealt to fellow Nigerians who had followed in my footsteps for the refining touch of my *alma mater*. It proved, as nothing else could, that the last place where one should expect to find Africans spoon-fed with the milk of English scholastic refinement was in Africa. Theoretically some of these products had been perceived to have developed a grossly inflated sense of their own importance (aka 'snobbery'), and to have an expectation of life that an African society could never hope to meet. They were perceived in terms of a burgeoning middle-class deadweight in

African society, their essential function being that of parasites – expensive, debilitating and deadly.

One of them died in his Nigerian environment aged just 22 from drink and stress-related illnesses. Another was tied to a tree and flogged at the behest of a serving military general for some undisclosed misdemeanour, and died in due course from depression. Yet another disembowelled himself and died in his father's mansion on Lagos island aged only 25. Another, a half-caste, also committed suicide. Yet another had to be confined in a strait-jacket after he stormed out of his car and engaged a bad driver and his three passengers in a raucous punch-up. He was overwhelmed by the weight of superior numbers, and went on to die at the age of thirty from drugs and depression.

I would soon encounter a childhood family friend with whom I had travelled to England at around the same age, going through the prep school and public school grooming processes with him, both of us spending many years in professional practice in London. We returned to our Nigerian homeland at about the same time, my friend managing his revered father's big-time printing business, the author trading in the book industry.

Ultimately the frustration of the system, the high-octane criminality, fiddling, sharp business, crass dishonesty, fraud and general corruption, overwhelmed my friend, and he was rushed out of the country with chronic cardiac illness, to be saved in the USA. It was touch and go, and he was lucky to survive. From there he relocated to his former UK base and lived in semi-retirement, but never fully recovered from his culture shock in Nigeria.

None of the foregoing beneficiaries of English education could fit into the African scheme of things in spite of the immense family wealth at their disposal. Clearly it was not a challenge that good education and big money alone could solve. Traumatized, saddened and depressed by the news of these tragedies, I was wont to ask myself, *why have you been so lucky? Why are you still here? How did you do it? How have you survived for so long?* I compared my people to a swarm of bees – inexorable, overwhelming reason driven by the sheer weight of stubbornness, ambition, energy and madness, inflicting many mental stings in the desperation to outsmart competition. Here is a nation which gives no room to intellectual power or the force of reason. Yet, for all the uncompromising drive and entrepreneurial spirit that regulate these remarkable people, one finds it impossible to expend any destructive emotion without feeling some measure of grudging admiration for their nerve. They can never, and will never, just lie down and say, "God help me." Rather – let everybody die together!

As you crave an opportunity to travel out for fresh air, and such an opportunity presents itself in the cabin of a modern jetliner in an acute climb skywards. As you look down at the ocean of flickering lights being left behind in the darkness on earth, your sense of relief wanes cold with guilt over your seeming 'abandonment' of your country. Occasionally there comes the murderous desire to machine-gun sanity into the whole population, yet you nurse a sense of outrage and sympathy for every victim of police brutality and extra-judicial killing that scorches the eyes and the senses. The system plays havoc with one's emotions. Here are the smartest and toughest people in the world in the challenge of survival. They will always find a way to circumvent every obstacle, dodge every rule.

Recall the example cited earlier whereby the Government, during the celebrations for FESTAC, tackled the traffic problem in Lagos by making it law that cars beginning with odd and even numbers be used respectively on alternate days, and the wealthy Nigerian citizen got round it by simply acquiring two cars. The chronic challenge of criminality, where armed robbers would invade homes in the early hours and rob wealthy residents, was circumvented by the hiring of private round-the-clock security. The super-rich amassed a private army of bodyguards to check the excesses of renegade soldiers who carried out assaults on individuals in their private homes. The bodyguards of one such powerful magnate were reported to have engaged an attacking group of renegade soldiers, beat them black and blue and carried them almost lifeless to the police station in a van. The soldiers were summarily dismissed from the military.

The 'cultural' purgatory of power outages was addressed by the purchase of generators and plants. The notorious disappointments suffered over the 'over-weighted' national airline (it was nicknamed 'the flying elephant' and soon ceased to exist) were checked by a proliferation of private airlines. The dangers posed by wealth and rivalry were combated by the hiring of full-time bodyguards, sometimes police personnel when the force became more commercialized. Hence the most notorious criminals could hire police protection.

The perennial water shortage was overcome by the digging of wells and boreholes, followed by an abundance of water-tankers to provide lucrative home delivery services.

The scandalous services provided by Government hospitals were compromised by the sprouting of private clinics. They charged exorbitant prices, but offered quicker and more efficient attention.

The flagrancy of the sale of justice was sounded eloquently in my ears when my lawyer in a civil case which I was destined to win asked me, "And how much are you going to bring for the Judge?" I won my case with a new lawyer and a new Judge, and did not pay a dime in bribes. Justice was for sale, favour was for sale, goodwill was for sale, one's happiness was for sale, sanity was for sale, and somehow fresh air was for sale. An unhealthy scenario emerged comparable to the rise of a Nigerian equivalent to Japan's Samurai warriors, where super-rich kingpins reared their heads with sufficient proficiency in power-play to compete and protect themselves, even against the government if the need arose. There were a lot of weapons in a lot of hands, procured mainly from politicians who had relied on the use of thugs to try and bulldoze their way into power.

But is it really as bad as all that, I ask myself in confused bewilderment? Is it really a situation of all tears and no laughter? Is there no redeeming feature? We look around in an effort to supply a positive answer, but see almost nothing – with the exception, that is, of that round man-made phenomenon called Money. Being round, it invariably rolls away, and our people are possessed of a devilish urge to catch it. Whatever virtues they may possess are lost in that frenzied rush, all morals thrown to the wind. And they hate each other because they are all bent on the achievement of the same singular objective.

Yet, at the end of the day, the African 'maniac' will always defer to the seniority of age, and extend the respectful greeting, "Good morning [or afternoon, or evening] sir." He will say it, in obeisance to the custom of the land, every day, without fail, to the same person. No African adult will ever answer him with an abrupt, "Look, will you please mind your own business."

At the end of the day, we have to laugh in order to not to die, a laughter fraught with the terrible anguish of the tormented, the insane, a laughter that has dried up our tears, somehow opposing the Nigerian journalist Peter Enahoro's literary work *You gotta cry to laugh*. It is only after careful reflection on that humorous philosophy that one starts to recognise, of necessity, the safety valve that humour can offer in a society such as ours, its power to defuse tension. So when I wonder, as I often do, how I have survived my people's ways without turning into a deranged moron, or expiring altogether, I duly recognise that by virtue of that British exposure to the value of humour, I have come to terms with a situation where my best moments are spent with myself, in the role of spectator, in a struggle to be able to see the funny side of a life which is anything but funny.

Yet, in a quirk of fate which one can only attribute to the mysteries of life, the relief of real, hearty laughter, like a heat-relieving breeze, brought me to a new dimension of happiness and pride to be a Nigerian. It came through a quarter which, by the very nature of its existence in this Third-World part of Mother Earth, would have been the least expected source of such a gracious act of Providence. By its very nature, in fact, it was ordinarily a source of disruption to life, a source of fear and quaking subservience, reflecting one of the remarkable ironies of life. It came from the Nigerian Military.

CHAPTER 15

An invasion of khaki

Truth! A monstrous entity that haunts my people like the fiery eyes of Satan in the darkness. Its voice chills their hearts like the occult growl of the living dead. They have declared it their greatest foe. Its glare penetrates the resilience of the African with a touch of terror. No conflict have they waged so relentlessly as the duel against Truth. No common threat has amassed such solidarity among Nigerians as that posed by it, and they have successfully checked its advance. A military junta outlawed it with Decree No. 4, prohibiting any unfavourable media exposure of those in power, truth being no defence. Hardy journalists tried to call their bluff, and became guests of federal prisons. One journalist sought to blackmail a military regime with the exposure of unspeakable truth, and was letter-bombed into oblivion. The literary matadors of *Newswatch* magazine decided to take the bull by the horns, and were badly gored and put out of action for six months when their magazine was closed down.

The rest of the Nigerian population have since been tamed. Silence became the new religion of the good, commanding a huge followership. But beneath that silence a war was being waged, fuelled by the aura of defiant Truth, which had been playing a sort of Mandela, undaunted, rejecting defeat, aware that the hour was almost at hand for what James Baldwin (of blessed memory) might have called *The Fire Next Time*. Yesterday the fire was called *Biafra*, and no lesson appeared to have been learnt from it. Next time?

For now the Nigerian people seemed content to wallow in the self-delusion of a positive course, scarcely aware of the escalator transporting them the opposite way to an unknown destination. And when they collapse in a heap, back from where they started, their efforts frustrated, their potential warped by the apparent hopelessness of the situation, on whom do they farm the blame? Evolution. They find it expedient to point to their rudimentary Third-World status, and dream and say "All in good time…"

But who really cares any more? In the absence of an incentive to create the basis for real development, might it not be a contradiction in terms to concern oneself about the vanquished principle of Truth when the unofficial green light has been given to go out and grab for oneself what one can – as if that is one's only hope? When the people's law tacitly prohibited Lord Queensberry from refereeing the tactics employed in the fight for survival? When the churches and mosques have failed to convince the people that the Almighty has not abandoned these parts, carting Truth away with Him?

They are all there, in all shades of human endeavour, self-appointed apostles using their distorted shades of Truth as mesmerising strategy to grab what they can, contributing to the dismay, confusion and ultimate anarchy that threatens to be the remedy. Applause for the observation of Theodor Herzl (of blessed memory) when he observed: "a man who invents a terrible explosive does more for peace than a thousand wild apostles". Yours Truly recognises that his country is comprised of wild apostles preaching everything but the truth. Their rulers have groomed Diplomacy as a substitute. So let one also applaud the succinct observation by Ludwig Boerne, the 18th-century German writer: "That two diplomats can look at each other without laughing amazes me."

The day two diplomats laugh in such a situation, Truth would cease to be Africa's foe.

At around 7 am on the last day of 1983, the shrill of my telephone wrenched me from the depths of blissful sleep. In irritation I strode over to answer – to be met with the ecstatic joy of an uncle.

"Have you heard the news?"

I had not.

"The army has taken over."

Suddenly I was pitchforked into life. Disbelief took over. "Are you serious?"

He was very serious. I slammed down the receiver and awoke the household with news of this thunderbolt, then stormed out on to the balcony to give the world applause. It was like manna from Heaven. Over four years of plunder, thievery and deception by the governing political power, and another prospective four years of purgatory at the hands of the same party (with wholesale rigging at the polls), had now been cremated by the men-of-arms.

The whole world appeared to share my glee. For the next seven days of honeymoon between the newly-weds, the civilians and the military, the divorced politicians were castigated with the stigma of Devil's Disciples, and their incarceration became a *cause célèbre*.

But upon reflection, I was of the view that the public's jubilation should be treated with caution. Did our people really know what they wanted? Had we not seen all this before? First the British colonists were the arch-villains, and the music of their withdrawal 'Highlifed' by the people (Highlife being a popular form of Nigerian folk music). Then the indigenes entered to steer the ship of independence, and before long they had taken the new Nigerian ship off course and on to the rocks. Screaming for their heads, the people waltzed to the martial music of the soldiers, who subsequently dismissed the civilian politicians with bloody barbarism.

Then after thirteen years that witnessed three coups and a civil war, the re-emergence of the civilians for another spell at the helm produced the familiar *danse macabre* from the people. And now, four years later, the dice of the roulette had once again stopped before the military players. So what next? How long now before one became tired of marching to martial music?

The military riders this time rode the Nigerian Bronco with a heavy-handedness never seen before, and for the first time the Bronco was tamed, cowering before the upraised whip poised to draw blood from flesh if she did not conform to the dictates of the uniformed rider. The hoarse cries of stubborn defiance, for which the Bronco had been well known since her discovery by the British hunters, had now been replaced with pathetic brays of subservience.

There had now been put in place a War Against Indiscipline (a name designed to sound like WHY). The popular culture of jumping queues and turning a deaf ear to the protests, most notably in traffic hold-ups, eased almost as if by magic at the abrupt materialisation of soldiers hidden from sight just waiting for the mortal sinner to commit abomination. The public would then be presented with the unholy drama of erring motorists being hauled out of their cars by deranged soldiers mouthing profanities, savaged with endless lashes of the horse-whip, made to perform frog-jumps on the kerb, kicked, rifle-butted and abused. Political looters of the Treasury became guests of federal prisons in lengthy sentences which, in some cases, reached 20 years, and several died from their ordeal. Drug-traffickers were executed by firing squad.

There is no denying that the Bronco was not happy, for the severity of its breaking was extreme – such that she and her civilian followers began to regret the dismissal of their previous civilian handlers. Newspaper houses were the most vocal in the expression of outrage, because Truth had been outlawed by military fiat.

Unfortunately for the hierarchy of the Supreme Military Council, dissent rose from within its rank and file – caused by an unhealthy development that brought echoes of The Charge of the Light Brigade, when 600 soldiers rode into the valley of death because one of their own had blundered. To obviate the disgrace of exposure and retirement, the blunderer instigated another change-of-batons within the ruling military council barely two years after the initial take-over. The early morning bulletins once again awoke the nation with the news a change of guard.

Thereafter something akin to a bizarre series of 'musical chairs' presented the Nigerian Bronco in its truest perspective – that the challenge of the Nigerian problem was irremediable. The facts spoke for themselves. The Bronco overthrew the first civilian prime minister after independence, together with three regional governors and a minister, hurling them to their deaths while they were still in office. Subsequently the first military administrator, together with his hosting military governor, were likewise killed in office. His military successor was ousted in a coup, followed by another military dictator who was subsequently assassinated in office.

A US-trained soldier then recorded a first by becoming the military administrator who survived in the saddle and dismounted of his own accord. The first civilian government after him was ousted in a coup. The subsequent military administration that replaced it was also ousted in a coup. Its military successor was forced to step aside.

Its civilian interim successor was outlawed by the courts, and forced out by the military. The following military successor died in office under questionable circumstances. A military 'midwife' to oversee a transition to civilian democracy was allowed just nine months to get out of the saddle.

The first earlier khaki general to survive the bloody musical chairs had now transformed into *agbada* (the traditional flowing robes of the Yoruba ethnic group), mounting the saddle, and once again showing himself to be master of the game. He handed over to an elected winner who died in office from stress-related health challenges, doubtless amplified by the anxieties of office. His successor was booed out of office after his first turn in the saddle. He was now followed by an earlier ousted military general, who had also transformed to *agbada* and was, like his predecessors, placed on a throne of bayonets.

From the foregoing examples it is clear that the people of Nigeria have expended more energy in killing their law enforcers that in obeying them, refusing to honour their leadership with the requisite followership that would have created the basis for a viable society.

It is a striking tribute to bitter irony that the military's misadventure into the affairs of state, on the excuse of coming to correct a harm, at the end of the day did more harm than good – almost to the point of upsetting the Nigerian applecart altogether. In a clear move to camouflage its academic bankruptcy, laid bare from time to time by threatening "anybody caught doing this shall be ruthlessly dealt with", the military destroyed the middle class, thereby triggering Nigeria's eternal brain-drain crisis, which saw our coveted population of European well-trained indigenes flee to the offshore sanctuary of Western civilization. Thereafter mediocrity was enthroned in "our own dear native land", paving way for the military, with the power of the gun, to establish the unspoken decree of "do as we say and not as we do". In consequence members of the military triumphed as some of the world's wealthiest billionaires, with less refinement than the nation's crude oil.

The hangman's noose of 'debt burden' has since hung around Nigeria's neck. Even with the withdrawal of soldiers to the barracks, the murderous do-or-die civilian elections for the corridors of powers have been fired by the single motive to go and grab. Such remains the national mind-set – to apply the rules of politics in the bedlam to survive. More blood has dripped from the exercise, more lives taken, than the mind can conjure up. It seemed as if only the Deity could provide the curative pill for sanity to reign.

Ironically it was during military rule that a more wholesome façade was presented to Nigeria's battered image in the eyes of the world. The most draconian junta in the history of military rule was that of dreaded strongman General Sani Abacha, who seized power on the 17th November 1993 in the last successful and bloodless *coup d'état* that Nigeria experienced. He was the first Nigerian army officer to attain the rank of a full military general without skipping a single rank.

Dubbed a kleptocrat and a dictator by modern commentators, Abacha did, admittedly, oversee the achievement of several economic feats. Those, however, were overshadowed by the global power of football, when Nigeria's dream team, the Super Eagles, became global icons during the Summer Olympics of 1996. Against all the odds, they took home the gold cup – the first time in history. It was a triumph that involved defeating the best soccer teams in the world at the time – Brazil and Argentina. Players and fans forever recall that feat as not just a victory for Nigerians, but one for Africans as a whole.

Football thereafter became Nigeria's national heartbeat, a new religion that drew everybody into its fold with a frenzy and fanaticism that eclipsed all other essentials of life outside money. The dreaded General Abacha played to the gallery with a handsome reward to each member of the Super Eagles, and to other Nigerian athletes who had triumphed in their respective sporting competitions. The reward for each sportsman combined big money and landed property on a scale of generosity that left the nation agog. The General was transformed overnight from a disciple of Satan to a modern Messiah. The seven-figure largesse in cash and landed property were like forerunners of a Government policy to offer incentives to bring out the best in a man. Football trod corruption underfoot, almost kicking it out of sight, out of reckoning. Everybody was suddenly proud to be Nigerian, fired by a new verve to go out and flourish and somehow showcase more talents from Nigeria to the world. A new Nigeria had been born.

As General Abacha basked in the glory of his nation's football triumph, his appalling human rights abuses and various political assassinations were swept under the carpet for the time being. They were compelled to resurface on March 22, 1998, when Pope John Paul II flew into Nigeria to implore him to release dozens of political prisoners locked up in degrading conditions.

Before Nigeria's football triumph at the Olympics, nearly all Western nations had shunned Abacha because of his government's political repression, most notably the 1995 execution of environmental activist Ken Saro-Wiwa and four others despite worldwide appeals for clemency. The country's gold medal at the Olympics served to give him a much-needed breather. The Pope's visit was timely, catching the General in an amiable mood following Nigeria's gold cup sensation, and then the national adulation over his largesse to the victorious sportsmen.

The Pontiff's visit was good timing indeed, as the General could not afford to allow his newfound popularity to wane. The Pope was by far the most prominent foreign visitor since Abacha had taken power. Doubtless this consideration, together with the status and office of the Pope, humbled this military strongman into immediate acquiescence to the plea of mercy for the incarcerated political activists, who were summarily released.

All was forgiven. Abacha was now a saint. A new meaning to life had been infused into the Nigerian system. The ugly core that harboured the cryptic cause of Nigeria's impossible drift into the jungle of Third-World chaos had now been discovered and destroyed. For the first time the principle of incentive had been introduced into the corridors of power. Latent invaluable talent could now be exposed through this new nation-building approach of rewarding excellence. Now everybody had been tacitly, spiritually, motivated. A new chapter towards the development of a super-nation had been opened, and incentive was the novelty which would determine the quality of the story-telling and form the plot-structure of the developed storyline. It had originated from the inadvertent Midas touch of a dreaded military dictator who had applied the whip to reposition a lost generation. From evil had come good. It was like the surprise sprung at the end of storyline that twisted and turned in the process of a tricky plot structure.

CHAPTER 16

The wise men from the east

"Think not that those are purely sages
Whose beard and pouch are large of size
Or else the goats through all the ages
Must, too, be classed among the wise."
- *Isaac ben Jacob, Jewish poet: 1801-1863*

The group of Nigerians from which Yours Truly is sprung deserves singular mention for its people's remarkable and complex nature. The disarming charm of their innate hospitality to a stranger would find few rivals among other human groups in the world. Their receptiveness and spontaneous wit have an instantly reassuring effect on a newcomer. Enriched by a culture of trading, they are blessed with an eagle-eyed business acumen and resourcefulness that attract the envy of their fellow ethnic groups in the Nigerian state. Add to those qualities their adroitness in the fine art of survival, enhanced by their adaptability to every situation, and one is presented with a people whose very existence represents (or should represent) a golden asset in the aspirations of the nation as a whole.

Yet, these attributes notwithstanding, my aged grandmother once passed this remark: "In as much as I have never travelled outside Nigeria, I am satisfied that there is no other group of people in this world as *bad* as our own Igbos."

A business tycoon extracted from that same group of people, having aged prematurely from stress-related challenges at the hands of his kinsmen, and watched his empire crash like splintered glass around him from the criminal guile of his Igbo staff, expressed his exasperation to me with undisguised venom: "There is something genetically wrong with the Igbo man!"

The Igbos of the East must be the most uncompromising and irrepressible group of people in the world. Put three Igbo political stalwarts in one room and they will form four political parties. But the Igbos remain birds of the same feather when it is a question of money. The other two main ethnic groups (the Yoruba and the Hausa) will die, respectively, for politics and for religion, but the Igbo man will die for money. The story goes of a bishop during mass requesting a $500,000 donation to assist the church. Of the three Igbos in the congregation, one promptly fainted, and the other two hurriedly carried him out.

I have witnessed endless raucous brawls between conductors and passengers, traders and customers, in disputes involving just a few dime. The political terrain has been littered with uncountable corpses of political rivals in disagreement over how to divide the spoils from thuggery. Igbo land surpasses all the other states in its obsession with recording profit, possessed as they are of the conviction that money is the essence of life, and hence one must be willing to do anything for it. That same money has been the most common cause of rivalry, even sibling rivalry, in Igbo land.

The Igbos fit no pattern. They are total non-conformists. Every

Igbo man is a king unto himself. If they have ever heard of humility, they are not likely to admit it. Ever since the Nigerian state was fused into a Federation in 1912, they have insulted, outraged, annoyed and captured world attention with their bombast and arrogance. They have persistently guyed and sent up their competitors and opponents in the Nigerian 'market'; they have baited them, chaffed them, bruised them with their often outrageously funny ripostes and assessments of their 'puny' potential against their almighty, all-conquering skills. Among themselves each Igbo knows what the other knows, each knows every trick in the rule book of survival; but in the system of healthy (or unhealthy) competition, each will be scheming to out-flourish the other in the world's public gaze. Each will often choose to be wrong for the sake of being different. Family meetings will be conducted with fiery, almost combative, exchange of discord and abuse, with voices raised to high heaven. For other Nigerians, the same sort of fearful dread felt by the locals in that famous horror classic is applicable to how the Igbos are viewed – Count Dracula has risen from the dead.

The Nigerian civil war, triggered by breakaway Igbos to form their own sovereign state of Biafra, not only laid bare genocidal designs against them but represented the appropriate stake to be driven through the hearts of these eastern Nigerian 'vampires' in order to guarantee their eternal demise. But it appears they emerged conquerors even of death, Dracula's African equivalents.

The Igbo bear the stigma throughout Nigeria and beyond of being the most hard-hearted group of people in the world, and even amongst themselves they recognise this unfavourable characteristic. The cunning and exceptional resourcefulness of the Igbo combine with their die-hard disposition to make them the most feared and mistrusted group of citizens in the Nigerian state. Their tendency to overshadow everybody and everything in the system of individual initiative has effectively permeated the whole of Nigerian society with Igbo 'blood', so that the 'blending' of the nation's many ethnic groups into one mass effort of solidarity has created an overriding Igbo 'complexion' in that unity. That complexion is easily discernible from the controversial aspects of the Nigerian character (which overshadow any favourable quality except, perhaps, hospitality) – namely guile, greed, corruption, treachery, malice, aggression and deceit.

In consequence, they are the people who invariably get the rawest deal in Nigeria. Their innate hospitality is usually regarded by members of other ethnic groups as a snare, like a crocodile's smile, to trap the unwary visitor and rob him through cunning; and having regard to their notoriously capitalist disposition, they must bear much of the blame for the corruption of the Nigerian character, the despoiling of such inherently guileless groups as the Hausas of the North, and the touch of insecurity with which the other ethnic groups view the prospects of competing against them in any sphere of life. One should now begin to have an idea of what the savagery of the Biafran war was all about, with its genocidal mission against the Igbo.

On returning home in 1981, I found it extremely difficult not to believe that the Igbo had become their own worst enemies, with little justification for grievance over the prison of mistrust to which they had been relegated in Nigerian society. It became further evident that while contending with their back-seat position in Nigeria, most Igbos will quickly develop a feeling of jealous resentment against progressive elements from within their own group, and will go the extra mile to sabotage that progress in order that misery may be blessed with company. Clearly self-hatred is the Igbo man's patriotism. It is a striking fact that most of the returning Nigerian

Been-Tos who gave up the fight for re-integration and fled back to Europe, or died 'before their time', or surrendered to debilitating ill-health, were drawn from the Igbo stock.

The late African-American General Colin Powell, in a fit of exasperation, publicly denounced the people of Nigeria in unedifying terms when he said, "They really are the most marvellous scammers. It must be in their culture." He was compelled to apologise in the wake of the explosion of outrage expressed by the people of Nigeria through the press. Yet what did he say wrong? It was no more than the painful truth. The anger of most Nigerians was centred on the fact that notwithstanding their guileless and well-meaning disposition, they were being held accountable for a kind of crime that was notoriously spearheaded by – wait for it – the wise men from the east! Intelligence reports from the Nigerian state security network fingered the Igbos as the number 1 scammers in the country, followed by a sprinkling of patrons from the Yoruba. Every imaginable kind of scam, from cheap imitation of all and any consumer goods to clothes, fake drugs, fake currency, fake ATM cards, book piracy, enjoyed the smart patronage of 'eastern' promise.

What share of hell I encountered in my fatherland was more among my Igbo kinsmen than any other ethnic group. Indeed, in terms of opportunity, what profit accrued from business pursuits, what plum government positions and contracts were availed to me, came from the goodwill of other groups.

The formidable strength of the genus Igbo, as one man, was endorsed in the research findings of Professor Elizabeth Isichei in *The History of the Igbo People*, in which she reports: "No Nigerian people resisted colonialism more tenaciously than the Igbo. The great Emirates of the north, once conquered, supported the British, with the minor exception of the Satiru rising. The conquest of Igbo land took over twenty years of constant military action." Moreover, it is a historical fact that one of the greatest challenges encountered by American black-market traffickers of the Western slave trade was the Igbo slaves who opted for suicide by diving into the ocean rather than be taken captive.

These glaring examples of die-hard defiance speak true of the same rejection by modern-day Igbos against any laid-down policies that constitute a hindrance to their God-given attributes. You fight them, you fight to the finish. There is no compromise. When one hears the common declaration that the Nigerian problem is insoluble because the Nigerian spirit is exceptionally difficult to break, one does not need to stretch one's imagination to fathom which group of people personifies the main subject of reference – the wise men from the east!

This point draws compelling attention to the 'Biafra' imbroglio. No evidence of African capability unsettled the Western powers more than the achievements of the Igbos in the course of that war. It was not for nothing that the combined strengths of the Kremlin and Whitehall found a common ground on which to take the unusual step of assisting Nigeria's tortuous, impossible efforts to break the Igbo resilience on the battlefield. Even with that unity, the 24-hour "police action" predicted by the Nigerian leadership did not overcome the Igbos; it required a protracted two and a half years of warfare that saw many Igbos, in the face of a land, sea and air blockade, reduced to the use of machetes and bows and arrows when push finally came to shove. In the absence of sustained supplies of effective firepower, they were forced to rely on their innate tenacity to defy the might of Europe, ready to die to the last man but for the timely intervention of a non-Igbo Colonel to call a truce on behalf of beleaguered Biafra.

From the standpoint of the European powers, the unwise decision to allow the Igbos to exist as a national entity was based on three considerations. In the first instance, oil would have been in their possession, making them a financial force to be reckoned with. The problem there, from the point of view of Western security, was that the most dangerous people on earth would constitute that financial force. It was no secret that the Caucasian powers gave grudging recognition to the high intelligence and resourcefulness of the Igbo.

Nothing exemplified the validity of such recognition more starkly than the events of the Nigerian civil war, when the Igbos were able to create original weaponry which, for a while, was put to effective use against the advancing federal troops. The tanks, rockets and bombs they built caused extensive damage during bombing raids and assaults, even inside enemy territories, paralysing Lagos International Airport for forty-eight hours.

Never before had there emerged a group of black indigenes that demonstrated the capacity to invent and create sophisticated weaponry without the assistance of a developed nation. It followed that if Igbo scientists could devise such weaponry under the stifling pressures of warfare, it was only realistic to recognise that in an era of peace, as an independent entity blessed with the Herculean financial power of oil, it would only be a matter of time before perseverance rewarded them with the open-sesame of ultimate scientific discovery – the secrets of the atomic weapon which could annihilate mankind. Such a state of affairs, attained by a group of people forever derided by European supremacists as inferior, would have been disastrous to the Western social order.

The immense power the Igbos would have wielded in Africa as an independent entity was recognised and feared by the West; and, of course, a well-armed, well-trained Igbo army would have caused more than a few goose-pimples in Western and South African military quarters. Those reasons were the be-all and end-all of the Soviet and British intervention in that war: all else is detail.

There is no doubting the very real existence of an unspoken policy that has prohibited a President of Igbo extraction from holding the reins of power in Nigeria. The grapevine has been rife with rumours of a secret resolve taken by the hierarchies of the other ethnic groups, allegedly instigated by the British, to adopt this policy as punishment for having the gall to almost break the country in two. It was further rumoured that this befitting punishment should have a 100-year duration. Not surprisingly, the Igbos have agitated against this suspected policy with hoarse cries of "marginalisation" that have never ceased to disorientate Nigeria's national eardrums. Certainly it is to their credit that defeat in their 'Biafran' initiative has had no adverse effect of a lasting nature (in spite of a casualty tally in the war that has been put at three million fatalities). They have emerged from that monumental drawback to push themselves forward in Nigeria's political power game. This irrepressible spirit might have its merits, but it exposes a self-destructive failure to fully digest the harsh lesson taught by the enormity of their defeat in the war. It called for greater circumspection in their dealings with the other ethnic groups, who remain unshaken in their rigid mistrust, bordering on hatred, of the genus Igbo. It called for some home-cleansing exercise, it called for a subtle approach, it called for 'conciliatory' steps to moderate their image of themselves as 'God's Chosen'. With such moderation, they would now properly appreciate why they are still running up a down escalator.

The issue is compounded by the volatile atmosphere inside the Igbo home itself, the unruly nature of the Igbo man, and the almost puerile factional dissension that prevails between various Igbo clans over who should hold the balance of power between them. If one considers the rabidity with which all the Igbos declared their solidarity in their bloody efforts to realise their 'Biafran' dream, is one really to accept that such unity is possible only at a time of crisis? The scale of in-fighting between the various Igbo sub-clans has degenerated to a farcical situation where some of them openly declare that they are not really Igbo at all, wanting to be accepted by the 'enemy'.

At the end of the day, in the seething welter of their frustration at being denied the Presidency of Nigeria, the Igbo nation has become divided between a sizable number (drawn from the youth) calling for the rejuvenation of the 'Biafran' dream – as against those who want to stay in Nigeria. The reasoning of the latter group is that having regard to the prevailing self-hatred as the Igbo man's patriotism, what guarantee would there be that the issue of leadership would not split the various factions and sub-clans, resulting in further agitations for separate developments?

It would be almost criminal not to touch on the story of the original fall of the Igbo man, even if briefly and sketchily. It was the Igbo who spearheaded, with indefatigable gusto, the fight for Nigeria's independence from the British, in the personage of a world figure nicknamed, for simplicity's sake, Zik. He became revered in due course by all of Nigeria's ethnic groups as 'Zik of Africa', rubbing shoulders with the likes of Nkrumah, Herbert Macaulay and Patrice Lumumba in the fight against colonial bondage. Aside from legendary pugilist Muhammad Ali, Zik must have ranked as one of the world's most charismatic human beings, always resplendent and imposing in his habitual white robes, red cap and chain of beads flowing down his chest, flashing his broad enigmatic smile as he expressed himself with eloquence that enriches his disarming mastery of the English language.

Zik loved the cultural wealth inherent in his country's conglomeration of ethnic groups, numbering some 400, the most diverse of any nation in the world. He became Nigeria's first Governor-General/Head of State during the colonial era, and later, in 1960, the first ceremonial President on Nigeria's independence.

In the subsequent two years of healthy romance between all the ethnic groups, Nigeria ranked high in the world public gaze as a model of peace and rectitude, in stark contrast with the bloody post-independence pogroms that bedevilled other nations south of the Sahara. I well remember my geography master at prep school in England, Mr. Gaussen, never failing to pause at the blackboard to speak highly of "that beautiful peaceful young nation Nigeria, in the West of Africa", which he would point out on the map.

As if all good things had to come to an end, hell disrupted the haven of peace that the Nigerian people enjoyed when a military coup was carried out by soldiers of mainly Igbo extraction. (In the series of accusations and denials that it was an Igbo-inspired coup, it has been practically impossible to sift the truth from the false.) As the case may be, the putsch saw the assassination of the Prime Minister (of Northern Muslim extraction), the Premier of the northern region (of Muslim extraction), the Premier of the Western region (of Yoruba extraction) and the Finance Minister (of mid-west extraction).

The soldiers invaded the residences of these revered leaders and shot and killed two of them at point blank range, then dragged out the Prime Minister and resisting Finance Minister, and later shot them and dumped them by the roadside. There was not one Igbo victim in the blood-letting of Nigeria's political 'sacred cows'. The President, the great Zik of Africa, had obviously been tipped off and was found to be resting in London at the time of the coup; otherwise, by rights, he should have been a victim, since he was an integral part of the administration that was marked for overthrow. The grapevine in due course presented a reason for the putsch as rooted in information that had become privy to the coup plotters of a plan by the Muslim north to Islamicise the Nigerian nation.

Later denials by Igbo interest groups that it had been an 'Igbo coup' calculated to entrench Igbo domination of the Nigerian state fell on sceptical ears, with dismissal from the other ethnic groups. It did not help that the Major-General who assumed power and quelled the take-over attempt was himself Igbo. Rather than court-martial the coup plotters and punish them with summary execution, and appease the aggrieved north by replacing the murdered functionaries with leaders from their respective ethnic groups, he decided to let sleeping dogs lie and took over the reins of power, enjoying the luxury of a Rolls-Royce conveyance in his motorcade.

There was a hideous backlash from northern soldiers. The Igbo Head of State was killed in a manner too gory to go into, followed by the systematic nationwide massacre of an estimated 33,000 Igbos. The northern military took over the reins of power, and citizens of the Igbo enclave seceded from the Nigerian Federation under the leadership of bearded Colonel Ojukwu, an alumnus of Oxford and Sandhurst. Nigerian oil was now in the control of the Igbo; and that fact, essentially, was the sore point in the gruesome 2½-year civil war that followed.

Would you begin to believe that during the post-war re-integration process, after the leadership of the victorious Nigerian side had sought to heal all wounds with its "no victor, no vanquished" jingle, rather than pursue a commitment to put their house in order and try to conciliate their enemies, the Igbos gave priority to pursuing a leadership struggle with daggers drawn to determine who would occupy the seat of 'Father of the Igbos'? Was it the great Zik of Africa, or was it the defeated Biafran warlord Colonel Ojukwu, who had personified leadership of the Igbos at a time of crisis? The crisis reached its climax during the 1983 general election. The brazenness of the rigging that took place therein left one open-mouthed at the audacity of it all, likewise the absolute barefacedness with which votes were swapped to give victory to losers, and many lives were taken in skirmishes on both sides of the political divide in Igbo land – to the amusement of the world at large.

Ojukwu declared himself 'King of the Igbos' *(Eze Igbo),* and Zik remained contented with his traditional widely-revered title '*Owelle*', which glorified his perceived greatness. Both personalities were almost stripped naked, dehumanised one could say, by the unspeakable character-assassination of their personage – by their own fellow Igbo followers! It had to be seen and heard at first hand to be believed. At the end of the day both great men lost in their bid for electoral victory, Zik for the Presidency, Ojukwu for a senatorial seat. No Igbo man was ever allowed the opportunity to win the Nigerian Presidency – they are still serving the sentence for the crime of secession. At the end of the day, still, the rabid mistrust felt by the other ethnic groups against the Igbo remains.

In the riotous whirlwind of ethnic and religious tensions that continue to flourish like jungle vegetation, the author has emerged miraculously unscathed, curiously unruffled, and blessedly untainted by that unhealthy scenario, enjoying a healthy respect from indigenes of all ethnic groups. He remains steadfast to the notion of his being favoured by the 'gods', and it is now his duty to lay bare the incredible irony of how he came to be blessed with such a miracle.

CHAPTER 17

Floreat Etona?

This motto of Yours Truly's *alma mater*, 'Floreat Etona', originated from an 1882 painting by Elizabeth Thompson, Lady Butler, meaning "May Eton Flourish". The painting depicts an incident that occurred during the first Boer War in 1881. Featured was Lieutenant Robert Elwes of the Grenadier Guards, who was killed on 28th January 1881 during the Battle of Laing's Nek. The British Army was attempting to bulldoze its way through a pass in the Drakensberg Mountains, where Lieutenant Elwes joined an ill-fated charge into the bared fangs of a formidable Boer Defence front. It was an uphill assault on horseback, and in the process he goaded a fellow Old Etonian who was adjutant of the 58th Regiment of Foot with a shout of, "Come on Monck! Floreat Etona! We must be in the front rank." The words had barely escaped his lips than he was shot and killed on the spot. He was among 83 fatalities, with 11 injured, but his old school contemporary Monck survived.

I did not encounter the deadly scale of warfare that characterised the Boer War on my homecoming, but the challenges by way of the traumatic effects of Third World life were not far removed from those of spending twenty years at a war front in one day. That I did not suffer the aforementioned fate of my old school predecessors and perish in the process was attributable, almost wholly, to the magical image of my *alma mater* in the world public gaze. The publication of my first book on Eton produced a wonder and intrigue in my country that was destined never to diminish, perhaps boosted by my people's awareness that it was worldwide news. Moreover, the reproduction of the initial two-part serialization of my story in Nigeria was followed by a six-part serialization of the actual book when it finally saw the light of day.

When I had attended the FESTAC celebrations, I had been in my element. On my final homecoming, I found myself in demand at almost every turn. My people were tickled by the concept of a true-life African aristocrat who had been bred at an elite college built by the British Royal Family. They were thrilled to bits, as reflected in the zeal with which he was introduced to the less informed as "the one who used to punch white people on the jaw". It beggared belief to so many that an African would summon such courage even here in Africa, let alone on the white man's own turf. It was also viewed as no less unthinkable that any African would have the audacity to pen such a damning indictment against the British aristocracy without some sort of retribution outside a mere ban, and still survive in the United Kingdom.

At that stage of their development, by and large they paid mere lip-service to the system of democracy (often satirically pronounced 'demo*crazy*' for emphasis of its eccentric application in this 'third' part of the world). The ban by my *alma mater* itself was, to them, like an additional crown to my head. My people were over the moon in their admiration, and accorded me something of a hero's welcome. From all the high praise emerged utterances which showed, as nothing else could, that many were still relatively ignorant of Western mores and behavioural patterns. There was the joy of introducing me, with emphasis, as "the Nigger", wholly unaware of the abusive message of the word in the context of its usage as a book title. Most people had not even heard the word. My final homecoming, with the boost of several well-publicised new books to my name, earned me the status of a celebrity, a public figure, just a few rungs below the pedestal. But I felt a touch of alarm over this hero-worship. As earlier observed, difficult things took a long time, the impossible a little longer. It seemed I was widely perceived as having the capacity to bring down the heavens. It was clear that most of my admirers had not read Charles Dickens' *Great Expectations*, and could not therefore appreciate that no man can be held responsible for what others expect of him. One could only try to act the part, relying on shrewd imagination, to apply the awaited English diction that was perceived to be peculiar to the Eton aristocracy, together with attendant mannerisms of finesse and good breeding, and with the finishing touch of English humility.

At the speaking engagements to which I was invited, it was no easy task to try to invent English words that could not be found in any dictionary, with abstruse sentences that paid tribute to intellectual sophistication that I did not possess, delivered like a philosopher of the very best school, higher even than my *alma mater,* to an audience that sat mesmerised in wonderment, ultimately to break out into an explosion of applause that threatened to go on for ever in worship of those magic words, precisely because nobody could understand them.

Eton paved the way to acquaintanceships with many eminent members of Nigeria's high and mighty. I was invited to meet the country's Vice-President at the then State House in Lagos, and showered with *bons mots*. In due course I was invited to the new capital, Abuja, by the Military President, with the request to be one of the launchers of the new Nigerian Handball Association. After the applause from the gathered dignitaries, followed by endless handshakes with the President, members of my Cabinet and the crème-de-la-crème of Nigerian society, I rushed back to my hometown base, Enugu (aka 'Coal City'), to make sure my cheque did not bounce.

I was subsequently fêted by State Governors, Ministers and business tycoons, and through such high-powered connections was awarded huge book publishing contracts that helped, in no small measure, to consecrate my business with one of the most prestigious names in the Nigerian book publishing industry. This enabled me to criss-cross tense religious boundaries to patronise and exalt members of the comparatively unlettered Muslim North with the favour of giving them life as authors of published books. In consequence I was blessed with many handsome publishing contracts from State Governments and business magnates from the northern part of the Federation. I became a distributor in Nigeria for several leading book publishers in the UK and the US.

It would not be an exaggeration to declare, with a strict regard for truth, that in terms of the publishing business (boosted significantly by new books penned from my ink but published offshore) that for Yours Truly it was forever smooth sailing. My publishing activities survived long after many of my competitors had gone off the radar. Eton College was responsible, in no small measure, for the plums and security that accrued.

My ego was boosted by the receipt of a Christmas greetings card from the Military President, notwithstanding the fact that he was a staunch Muslim. Through that connection I was able to secure a board appointment on the Government tabloid newspaper *Daily Star*.

More dividends came with the appointment, by the Abacha military government, of an appointment to serve on a nationwide five-man Committee of Local Governors to oversee the administration of my native Local Government Area. It was a fulfilling two-year experience in executive governance. In due course I would be the guest of a civilian president, invited to visit the presidential villa at Aso Rock, Abuja. I joined the President and eminent guests and members of his Cabinet for morning prayers before the day's government business, and was later entertained by the flurry of comings and goings of big-time political functionaries coming to meet with the President. The privilege was finalised by the additional glamour of being one of two of the President's special guests to join his mile-long presidential motorcade to the airport. From there it was on to his private suite in the Presidential Boeing 737, with a hop over by helicopter to the President's vast country estate. I spent the weekend in the President's luxurious villa, where I was treated to choice cuisine served by solicitous staff, enjoyed breakfast with the President and other visiting VIP guests, and held a private late-night discussion with him on strategies to move the country forward. The discussion followed in the wake of the President's expressed appreciation of my supportive written critique on his administration.

After the merits of the nation-building proposals had been discussed at length, the President asked me, "Would you be willing to come on board and serve the government as a Special Assistant on National Orientation?" I answered in the affirmative, expressing my appreciation of such an honour.

"Very well. I shall give you a job and an assignment. You will follow me to New York in two weeks to meet the new Secretary of the United Nations, Ban-Ki Moon."

Unhappily, after I was asked by the President's Special Adviser to present my CV ("otherwise you will not get paid"), which I always carried with him, and was told that I would be contacted in due course to come and start work, that was the last I heard about it. I later learned that I had been just another victim of the notorious in-fighting, cutthroat business and sabotage that bedevilled every opportunity that loomed for employment in the corridors of power. I was left in no doubt that someone privy to my potential appointment had sabotaged it, and in due course was presented with two names within the Government circle who had conspired to ensure it did not happen. One of them, not surprisingly, was an Igbo. I was made to understand that I was to blame for my loss. The President's frenetic schedules in the affairs of state, including but not limited to the mountain of briefs on his table to wade through, and the uncountable meetings and travel schedules with which he had to contend, made it well-nigh impossible for him to remember what he had said to whom, when and where, unless the aspiring 'job seeker' had a powerful connection who would continue to remind His Excellency. I had no such connection, having been accorded the privilege of meeting the President only through the vagaries of the hour. I was still too afflicted with 'English gentleman fever', and was made to understand that when such a golden opportunity reared its head here in Africa, I should not just sit on my ass and wait till kingdom come to be contacted; I should follow it up immediately and allow the President's Special Adviser assigned to follow the process no room even to breathe, let alone to rest, in pursuit of that looming golden dawn.

I took the loss in my stride, seeing it in terms of every disappointment being a blessing in disguise. But it was a privilege to have been fêted by the President of Nigeria, and I was to learn through the grapevine in due course that His Excellency had been inspired by my family background as the son of a former Nigerian International Court Judge and a product of Eton College.

All these pleasant experiences taking place in a developing Third-World milieu served to gradually diminish the lingering dreams of those glorious London days gone by, but never ceased to remind me of the good fortune of having been schooled at my almighty *alma mater*. It had been a saving grace that spared me the full purgatory of Third-World life, and from that perspective I have never ceased to be grateful.

But it was not always smooth sailing. Admirers there were in abundance, but so were avowed enemies. On returning to my hotel in the early months of my return home, a message was handed to me at reception with the words scrawled on a piece of paper, "If you are cut, you're going to bleed." It was a startling message, to say the least. The receptionist reported that the visitor who had left the message would not give leave his name, describing his physique as large and burly, and putting his age around the mid-20s.

There was indeed a security problem during those earlier days of Nigeria's oil bonanza, with a high rate of violent crime firing the get-rich-quick mania. My domination of the headlines did not blind me and my English better half to the dangers of presenting a target to kidnappers and armed robbers, hence the need for strict vigilance.

By a quirk of unbelievable coincidence, a visit later that evening to the residence of a former top-ranking diplomat who was married to my godfather's daughter exposed the author of the threatening note left at the hotel reception. He was actually an Old Etonian! He entered the parlour to say hello strapped in a straitjacket, his unsteady gait assisted by two adult housekeepers. His greeting was curt, and he wasted no time in confessing that he had gone to the hotel earlier that day armed with a knife, with murder in mind. He was a pitiful sight, a shattered mental case, tormented by demons. He shook his head repeatedly and cursed the Third-World status of Nigerian society, declaring that he could no longer survive here. He attributed the reason for his murderous intention earlier that day to the perceived good press with which I was regularly being showered, to his chagrin. He recounted that he had endured unbearable hostility at Eton as a result of my book. It had precipitated his running away from the school, triggering a scandal that hit the headlines at the time. After he had returned to the school, and the dust from his abscondment had settled, he had been persuaded by his contemporaries to denounce *Nigger at Eton* in a series of newspaper articles.

My better half calmed me down with words of comfort and reassurance, a new friendship with him was sealed, and life thereafter went on. Sadly he passed away a few years later.

It is a striking fact that the murderous designs that fuelled the young man's rage well reflected the seething welter of emotions in the criminal atmosphere and infighting that regulated Nigerian life. At its primitive extreme, murder motivated the ordinary yokel based on the mere *sight* of one's happiness, let alone success. Nigeria was a dangerous society that called for circumspection in one's utterances and movements, and one was chilled by the number of Been-Tos who were killed for no other reason than envy and insecurity. I stuck to the rule, to look, listen and say nothing. I wore my learning like a valuable watch, stowed away in a private pocket, on no account to be pulled out for the world to see. Even that policy held its risks of perceived snobbery, however tight the stiff upper lip. Enforced silence was interpreted as quiet contempt. The matter became a vicious circle when the more one handed out in bribes, or in goodwill gestures to the less privileged, the louder the tacit declaration of one's superior wealth, and the greater the general resentment.

Matters would be inflamed when unheralded and unsolicited visits to one's residence with the expectation of drinks and refreshments, and maybe monetary hand-outs, were settled with courteous dismissal at the front door. Suffice it to say that the generality of Third-World life, by virtue of the vast limitations sprung from its developing status, exhausted the Been-To over and above the profit he gained from entrepreneurial or political dividends. There was also a limit to which, in the worsening global recession, globe-trotting could offer relief. Moreover, because of the sense of guilt over the idea of abandonment that the regularity of such trips instilled in one, no trip abroad exceeded two weeks. As if possibly divining that policy, the relief and pleasure sought were reduced by an attendant sense of *déjà vu*. I had seen all there was to see in Europe.

From the analysis of good and evil, however, I had cause to smile. My exclusive breeding ground had provided a Midas touch to precipitate my good fortune; it enabled me to show tolerance, understanding and compassion towards the generality of my under-privileged countrymen. But I remain deeply saddened to have out-survived almost all those of my age group who had not experienced the privilege of an elite English education. At each funeral I was traumatised by the sight of the deceased lying in state preparatory to being lowered down into the dusty bosom of Mother Earth. Sometimes I was almost reduced to tears by lingering memories of our good times together in London.

For sure, I would have come to grief myself and been abandoned by my many admirers if I had elected to go into politics, for the Nigerian political arena saw man at his most savage and depraved, especially in his native Igbo land, where murder, kidnapping, torture, character assassination, treachery, fraud and vote-rigging all flourished like a terrible typhoon. "In this part of the world," a seasoned political observer told me, "politics is the devil's game. And the only time you can trust anybody is when you undergo an initiation ritual into a select group in a political party. You would be called upon to appear naked before your fellow members, swear an oath of allegiance, then have your hand slashed with a knife and held over a basin containing the blood of the other initiates. The blood would be swirled around to symbolise unity, a kola nut would be dipped into it, and then broken into pieces to be shared round and eaten. Once you eat it, the spiritual bond of trust has been sealed. Nobody would dare to break that trust for fear of supernatural retribution. Can you see yourself going through all that?"

I could not.

"Can you see yourself employing full-time thugs knowing that somewhere along the line they will have to kill opponents? Can you see yourself parting with millions of your life's savings to buy votes, not knowing whether you might lose those votes to a higher price by opponents?"

I was hesitant.

The other man went on, "And assuming you were elected, say, a Governor, could you see yourself awarding a contract of fifty million naira to your party members for a road that would never be constructed?"

He listed more examples of the devilishness awaiting one in the political arena, citing more examples of hideous blood-curdling sacrifices in which daredevils would engage in order to become rich. Squirming at the hideousness of what people would do to become rich, I declared that I would rather remain poor than be remotely associated with any of them. Every personal instinct rebelled at the thought of such sacrilege to my orientation.

But then it was not just the blessing of an Eton education that facilitated the ability to survive against overwhelming odds. We have seen that there were several cases where products from my *alma mater* went off the radar from the culture shock of attempted re-integration. It was the good fortune that accrued from having penned a book that transformed me into a hero among my people, bringing a scale of respect not accorded even to public figures who had been elevated to the most distinguished positions in the affairs of state. I had since bestraddled that enviable position of respect and acclaim like a Colossus. It had been a matter of sheer luck – and nothing else. Because, by rights, I should have gone under from the sheer weight of the challenges of survival in the Third-World milieu of my fatherland.

Floreat Etona!

CHAPTER 18

The anatomy of a repentance

It would not be wholly accurate for me to suggest that the present contains nothing more than the past, and what is found in the effect was already in the cause. Such a notion may be applicable in developed societies, but in my African environment, it was the ever-prevailing situation of an old 'mistake' in Europe becoming a new invention in Africa. In England one could imagine the past looking better than it was, but then it would seem pleasant only because it was no longer there. For the Englishman to look back into the past would be something like looking back to antiquity; but even if it were possible, there would be no immediate desire to want to go back there.

For me to say "goodbye Europe" and stand by it would be predicated on a rigid resolve against returning to old territory if I were to survive in the new, but arguably backward, milieu that was my place of birth. It had to be a decisive final resolve to say "Goodbye to all that" and become a true son of the soil.

I was satisfied that I had achieved success in this resolve once I no longer felt the urge to travel to the West, resolving that it would remain a lifelong policy provided unforeseen challenges beyond control did not emerge to necessitate such a trip. Even ill-health, one of the most common causes for wealthy Nigerians to seek relief offshore, was addressed with an inclination to make do with the comparatively skeletal medical services that were available on home soil. Being in the creative discipline of the written word and book publishing, I was able to apply creative measures to circumvent everyday challenges that were 'Third World' in nature, applying schooled tact, good sense and subtle evasive action to preserve blessed peace and keep my sanity intact.

When it appeared that my interest in matters European had dissipated with time and deliberate policy outside what such Cable TV networks as BBC, CNN, Sky News and Aljazeera had to report to keep one abreast with happenings around the world, a familiar but half-forgotten subject matter reared its head. A military junta that briefly came and went like a yoyo in the tiny West African state of The Gambia publicly castigated the growing popularity of sex tourism there. The villains were exposed as English wives torn by the woes of broken marriages and seeking the bedroom services of impressionable but brawny young Gambians, whom they would court with the physical magnetism of a modern Eve, with the additional incentive of a handsome honorarium. In several cases they would lure their new catch back to Europe and train them in the niceties of romantic love and caring for women.

"So those English chaps have run out of ideas, after all," I mused wryly. With the proliferation of 'battered wives' homes' in London, clearly every imaginable avenue of pleasure-enhancement on the love-couch had been explored beyond saturation point; and in the wake of the frustration and boredom that followed thereafter, the aggrieved husbands released their venom on their hitherto 'better halves'.

My thoughts on the matter, *vis-à-vis* the Gambian experience, was that those engrossments were best enjoyed in their natural European environment offshore to where those suitors would be taken. This was because the European was abnormally motivated by the pleasures of the flesh, and it seemed as if his overall outlook in life, and his physique, were specially designed to develop them into a fine art. Let the home-based African try to make his way in the celestial waters of comparative celibacy that abstinence has ushered in, and let the Holy Communion cleanse the willing spirit free from that weakness of the flesh except for purposes of procreation. Let Africa remain relatively innocent in that aspect of human weakness, in consequence representing one area of compromise that globalization will fail to secure in this part of the world.

In the wake of the media blitz on the new culture of foreign sex tourism in The Gambia, enterprising wizards in my homeland hit on the bright idea of carving out some of that lucrative business for themselves. The lovesickness afflicting the European, now characterised by broken homes and the collapse of the marriage institution following the unspoken relaxation of rules against adultery and the promotion of free love in general (with racial harmony just coming along for the ride), appeared to find a panacea in the new tradition of female European fishers of black men on the Atlantic beaches of The Gambia and Nigeria. At the end of the day, the alien experience of romantic love in an African setting was shown to represent the perfect bait for unsuspecting English ladies who had regarded their male African catch as signalling the end of their emotional-cum-sexual woes. Whatever qualities they detected in their younger lovers, their ability to fake it remained unnoticed. Only after it was too late, following a Houdini-type disappearance from the 'contracted' cohabitation, would it dawn that the Third-

World simplicity and innocence of the African male, enhanced by enrapturing charm, camouflaged shrewd and discerning eyes that saw beyond the magnetic beckoning of the mound of Venus and the ease of its owner's submissiveness to the moderate wealth which gave her security. In time that wealth would be gradually whittled away by the spell of his 'enslaving' love, ultimately filling his suitcase in his Houdini-like disappearance from her life. He left behind him a broken picture of emotional devastation, despair and financial ruin.

I was appalled to receive phone calls from sundry distraught white females, formerly my friends, who were desperate to trace the whereabouts of Nigerian lovers who had vanished with their life savings. The Nigerian public was riveted by the arrival of one such hysterical white American lady who cried through the media, reached out to the military, to the police, and finally to the First Lady, pleading vainly for their intervention to effect the arrest of a lover who had divested her of all her millions of dollars and fled back to Nigeria. In every case of woe, fictitious names and non-existent families and addresses in Nigeria had been used in the well-planned scam.

Such an army of 'fly-by-night' entrepreneurs represented a sizeable crop of Nigeria's *nouveaux riches*, uprooted from the fertility of the soil in the field of European love-life, becoming the forerunners of many young Nigerians eager to travel offshore either to date or marry white women of means. It became a lucrative enterprise.

The gentle, slow process of twilight, from early in the evening to late at night during the summer season in England, mirrors the gradual process of the English romantic love-game, in which it is savoured and relished as though it might never end. This is in contrast to my home scenario, the land of no twilight, in which, appropriately, there is also no love. As the African shark streaks through business waters towards the blood-scent of big money, so does the European lady demonstrate an obsession for the giving and taking of love. Both of them desecrate every emotional and biblical injunction. The African shark gets the better of both worlds, and morals have gone to the wind. Both have sinned, and the Good Lord is going to have a lot of judging to do.

A new epilogue is added with the collapse of the apartheid system in South Africa, whose black indigenes have now taken the reins of political leadership. The fear of a vengeful 'blacklash' has so unnerved the former oppressors that what was once unthinkable has become a new fashion. Wholesale surrender from members of the white female 'tribe' to black male partners in bedroom frolics, as apology for the sins of the apartheid fathers, now brings a stampede of hawk-eyed business lechers from all corners south of the Sahara to sample the special exotic flavour of the formerly forbidden apple, with an eye for possible business dividends accruing therefrom. "Gosh, is it on offer? Yes please!" they proclaim in disbelief as they race each other for the best of the spoils. The Dutch Reformed Church has further rehabilitated the stiffness of its earlier structured policies by accommodating this new 'alien' blend towards harmonization of its races.

Here, then, is the gold rush to the land of gold and diamonds. Where – need you guess? Both symbolically and physically, it is down south at the equator of the Aryan female anatomy, right at that juncture called 'the Cape of Good Hope' now that apartheid has been abolished, laying bare the golden *mons pubis* that shields the rich secrets of the warm caves on offer to the liberated 'Kaffir' miners. Forget all that humbug that if you bear too far down south in the Earth's crust, you'll reach hell. It's the opposite.

So the message is clear: the sinfulness of that system that sought to question the right of man's Maker to create people of midnight hue, as such dehumanising them for so many decades, could now be compromised by the sinfulness of bedroom frolics with bronzed female Europeans as compensation. Respect for the dignity of man is thus compromised by respect for dignity in beastliness. Let's make love, not war – right?

Dear God, whatever did you create? Still, let thy infinite goodness and mercy continue to prevail. Your spirit shall not forever strive with man. Repent ye not that you have made man on earth. Forgive us, for we know not what we do, and do not destroy the work of thine own hands. After all, love was the sole motivation behind your decision to shape us into being. You did nothing wrong with that decision, and there is nothing further that you owe the human being. The onus is on us to show ourselves to be worthy of all the blessings that we ask of You.

May Your Holy Name be magnified, exalted, and glorified above the heavens and the universe. Hallowed be thy name, Almighty Father.

ND - #0387 - 270225 - C1 - 216/138/12 - PB - 9781739864538 - Gloss Lamination